STEPS AND STAGES: FROM 3 TO 5

The Preschool Years

STEPS AND STAGES: FROM 3 TO 5

The Preschool Years

Holly Bennett and Teresa Pittman

KEY PORTER BOOKS

Canadian Cataloguing in Publication Data

Pitman, Teresa
   Steps and stages 3 to 5 : the preschool years

ISBN 1-55013-972-X

1. Preschool children. 2. Child development. 3. Child rearing. I. Bennett, Holly. 1957- . II. Title. III. Title: Steps and stages three to five. IV. Series: Pitman, Teresa. Steps & stages guides.

HQ774.5.P572 1998   649'.123   C97-932792-X

The publisher gratefully acknowledges the assistance of the Canada Council and the Ontario Arts Council.

Key Porter Books
70 The Esplanade
Toronto, Ontario
Canada M5E 1R2

THE CANADA COUNCIL   LE CONSEIL DES ARTS
  FOR THE ARTS   DU CANADA
  SINCE 1957   DEPUIS 1957

The poem "Dawdle, Dawdle, Dawdle" is reprinted from Jelly Belly by Dennis Lee ©1983 with permission of Macmillan Canada.

Printed and bound in Canada

98 99 00 01 5 4 3 2 1

Contents

Acknowledgements

THERE ARE ALWAYS SO MANY PEOPLE TO THANK, but, like a good speech, we think acknowledgements should be brief.

First and foremost, our thanks to the many parents and professionals who have shared their time, their thoughts and their experiences with children so generously and so often.

Second, to our own kids, who taught us most of what we know about parenting, forgave our gazillion mistakes and continue to make our lives interesting and fun.

Finally, we send our heartfelt thanks to Fran Fearnley, former editor-in-chief of Today's Parent Group, who took a chance on both of us over ten years ago, and has been a wonderful editor, mentor and friend ever since.

First Words

DELIGHTFUL THOUGH TODDLERS ARE, most parents heave a little sigh of relief as the third birthday rolls around. Yes, there are still plenty of bumps and challenges in the road ahead, but life with a preschooler is just, well, more *civilized*.

It happens almost imperceptibly. One day you realize: you can leave him in another room for a few minutes, without worrying about what he's doing. Although your poisonous cleaners are still locked away, your home no longer feels like a ship (everything battened down!). Bedtime has fallen into a routine that actually works pretty well, most nights. He can have a friend over for the morning and spend most of that time playing quite co-operatively, without much help from you. He talks a blue streak, demonstrating each day his growing ability to reason, imagine and remember. He feeds himself, dresses himself, goes to the toilet himself....

And still needs you as much as ever. True, there's less "physical maintenance" for you to do. But your preschooler depends on you to talk with her, show her how things work, teach her the skills and rules of living, applaud her new abilities, and help her feel secure and confident as she gets her first glimpses of how vast and varied the world really is.

Over the next few years, there will be times when your child is visibly growing in all directions at once, full of eagerness and independence. There will also be times when he seems to be "regressing"— when he will act inexplicably fearful, moody, demanding or clingy. That's a normal pattern for children; when growing up becomes a little overwhelming, a temporary step backward seems to help them prepare for the new steps forward to come. At these times, your child needs to know that you love him, absolutely and without question, even when he's being balky or babyish. That strong foundation of love and trust that you share is still the key ingredient—now and for many years to come—to your child's healthy development.

Holly Bennett

Teresa Pitman

New Skills, New Experiences:
Your Growing-up Preschooler

Brenda Cooke

THE CHANGE IS SO GRADUAL that most of the time our children's growth towards increasing independence and sophistication is imperceptible. But in the preschool years, there are moments that make you sit up and take notice: your child, so recently a devout messmaker, draws down her mouth in disapproval of a visiting baby who gleefully scatters his toys and food; you drop her off at preschool and instead of

1

your usual big smooshy hug, she gallops off to join her friend with a negligent "See ya!"; she joins you making cookies and is actually a help rather than a hindrance; she asks, "What happens when you die?" and you realize that a glib, simple answer just won't do. Your child is growing up.

He's not a "big kid" yet, though, and in moments of impatience you may sometimes have to remind yourself that his thought processes and emotional development are still very immature. Your three-year-old's social skills may crumble all too easily when faced with the demand to share his favourite bear. At four, his preoccupation with personal power may lead to sudden rages and aggressive behaviour, or even periods of clingy helplessness. At five he may well seem more easygoing and confident—but he still isn't likely to have the big-picture perspective that will allow him to understand why it's more important to catch a bus than check out a worm on the driveway, or the experience to really believe (although he "knows") that monsters are just pretend.

While many children today are well accustomed to daycare by three, the entry into school—whether nursery school or kindergarten—still marks a significant rite of passage. These are the first steps on a road that she will travel, largely without you, throughout her childhood. Although you are still her favourite company (usually), and although she needs to take things at her own speed, she is leaving babyhood behind and heading into the world.

"I CAN DO IT!": DEVELOPING SELF-CONFIDENCE

FOUR-YEAR-OLD JACK WAS EAGER to learn to swim—but he faced one big stumbling block. He was afraid to put his face in the water. His instructor, wisely, never bullied or forced him, but patiently encouraged. Then one day Jack took the plunge. In one lesson, he progressed from blowing cautious bubbles, to putting in his nose, to putting his whole head underwater. By the end of the class he had done a (very brief) unsupported front float—and he was deliriously proud. "I thought I couldn't do it!" he told his mom in the change room. "But you can do more than you think if you try."

Of course Jack has been learning new skills at a tremendous rate ever since he was born. But now, as a preschooler, he brings a new self-consciousness to his own learning process. And he is well on his way to developing a healthy confidence in his own abilities.

Toronto-area parenting instructor Susan Stuart is clear about the importance of developing self-confidence. "The self-confident child is willing to take some risks and try something new, and that adds to the child's enjoyment of life."

How can parents help children feel capable?

For preschoolers, with so much to learn, life can seem like one big challenge. An enthusiastic response from Mom and Dad to each small achievement can mean a great deal. Post her artwork on the fridge and take the few minutes to hear her count to ten (okay, so she missed the number seven, but she got all the others in the right order). Support her efforts as well as her successes: "Tying shoes is pretty hard for a four-year-old. But you made a good start with the first knot. One day, you'll be able to do the whole thing."

Confidence is increased as the child develops independence, says Stuart: "When you do things for the child that she can do for herself,

---

THE CHILD WHO IS SLOW TO WARM UP

When my daughter Lisa was three, her most noticeable characteristic was something I call "being slow to warm up." It took her a long time to get comfortable with new situations and challenges. If we went to a birthday party at a friend's house, she would sit on my lap for the first hour or so while she decided whether or not to join in. She *seemed* so much less confident than the more gregarious children who jumped right in.

I thought putting pressure on her would make things worse, and I was confident that she would do things when she was ready. So I let Lisa know I had faith in her abilities, and waited.

People who knew her then were surprised when, a few years later, she asked me if she could audition for a ballet school—and not only was accepted but thoroughly enjoyed the audition process. She's been an enthusiastic performer ever since.

For Lisa, the key was patience. In our society, we tend to see the extroverted people as the most self-confident. But kids (and adults) have all kinds of different personalities. Real self-confidence is not making yourself into someone different, but having faith in who you are.

---

you imply that you believe she's not capable," she says. A preschooler who can dress herself, call her grandma on the phone, or get herself a cracker has concrete evidence that she's growing up. "The same thing happens when parents plan or structure activities too much," adds Stuart. "It's as though the parents think the child can't do anything without a push from them." Instead, you can sometimes ask a simple question: "What would you like to do now?" or offer a choice: "Would you like to go to the park or the library?" when your child is "bored" and looking for entertainment.

"Too often we confuse caring with correcting," says Jody Orr, a teacher and music therapist. "It helps to step back and let the child figure out for himself what he's doing wrong, and how to fix it. If the boat he made won't float, don't give him a lot of advice, just let him try again. Solving the problem on his own increases his confidence."

Orr adds it is important that the challenges you ask your child to meet are not too difficult. "Learning to do something new is always a struggle, and children need ample opportunities to do things they already do well," she says. "Most of the time, they should be succeeding. That's what helps them develop confidence." Learning, she says, should be in very small increments so that the child will be quickly successful. She uses this technique in teaching music: at least 50 percent of the time the child works on music she already knows, and new music is introduced gradually, at a pace that suits the child. "You have to set things up that you know they can handle," Orr explains. "Many will just give up if the challenge seems too difficult."

Susan Stuart also recommends setting a good example. Can you laugh at your mistakes, and enjoy doing things even if you aren't good at them? For the preschooler who is overwhelmed by the number of things he's not capable of doing, it helps to know there are things Mom and Dad can't do well either. And he may like to hear your stories of trying, failing and eventually learning a new skill.

My youngest son, Jeremy, told me sadly at age five that he figured school was going to be pretty hard for him. When I asked him why, he said: "Because I can't read like you and the older kids." As we talked, I realized that he

MORE TIPS ON FOSTERING SELF-CONFIDENCE
A brochure for parents called *I Know I Can't Do It*, from the Canadian Mental Health Association, includes these suggestions:

• "Don't for one minute suggest that your love is linked to his accomplishments.... Confidence blossoms in a home that is full of love and affection. Love, security and acceptance are at the heart of family life."

• "When he's discouraged—'I'm really lousy'—let him express his feelings but help him see himself in a better light. Point out past achievements.... Encourage him to have fun doing what he enjoys, even if he isn't very good at it."

• "Self-confidence comes with meeting challenges—big ones and small ones. There are many ways to help your child develop a sense of accomplishment."

thought we'd all been born reading! After that conversation, I made more effort to help him see that we all struggle a bit as we learn new things.

Orr also reminds parents not to see self-confidence as "being conceited." What's wrong, anyway, with crowing, "I'm the awesomest runner!"

"Every child has some areas where they sparkle," Orr says, smiling. "So let them sparkle, and let them know how much you enjoy their achievements."

RULES RULE!: WHY PRESCHOOLERS ARE INTO LAW AND ORDER

OMETHING INTERESTING SOMETIMES happens along the road that leads a child into the preschool years. That rowdy, turbulent little bohemian suddenly embraces structure. He understands and accepts rules (most of the time). He *likes* rules. Likes them so much, in fact, that he makes up more rules than ever occurred to his parents.

Allan, a dedicated nudist throughout toddlerhood, at three bursts into outraged tears when his brother comes to lunch minus a shirt: "You have to wear *all your clothes* to the table!"

Corinne insists that not only all human passengers, but any travelling dolls and teddy bears, must wear properly buckled seat belts in the car.

Hannah becomes fretful and officious with her toddler cousin: "Dig the sand with the shovel, not your hands. No, just put it in the bucket! Mommy, James put sand on the grass!"

"Preschoolers are trying to make sense of the world, and familiar rules and routines allow them to predict what will happen," explains Janet Libbey, daycare co-ordinator for Canadian Mothercraft in Ottawa. "They need the sense of order and security that rules can bring."

That's partly why age three (or thereabouts) often brings a sense of relief to parents. While a preschooler is certainly still capable of vigorously asserting his own wants, he also seems to find satisfaction in meeting our expectations ("I did a good clean-up of my crayons, Daddy!"). The flip side is that he may cling rigidly to his *own* expectations of how things ought to be. "I remember my nephew at that age having a total breakdown if someone cut his toast in squares instead of triangles," says mother of two Janet McAulay. "His sandwich had to be prepared with the peanut butter *on top* of the jam, and the cutlery placed just the right way when you set the table."

GIRLS AND BOYS

The preschool fascination with rules and categories very often extends to sex roles, sometimes in a perturbingly rigid fashion:

- "Girls have long hair and boys have short hair," proclaims Stephanie, whose own mother has a short haircut and whose older male cousin sports a ponytail.
- "I really like those puppies," says Aaron, eyeing his young neighbour's collection of plastic dogs. "But I don't know if I can get one. It might be a girl's toy."
- "The boys don't play here in the kitchen centre," announce a trio of kindergarten girls. "Well, boys don't cook!"

It's sad but true; preschoolers often have strong sexist leanings. But there's no need to panic—this is just an expression of their need for clarity. To understand what makes men different from women, they may have to start with some rather crude oppositions. Some gentle corrections may be in order, but you don't need to be heavy-handed about it. You might remark on what a good cook Uncle Paul is, look at a picture book that shows how styles for men and women vary through history or in different cultures, and give your child clear encouragement to pretend or play with anything that interests her, regardless of what sex it seems aimed at. In general, as long as you continue to expose them to nontraditional possibilities, children's views will broaden as they mature.

Faced with such "unreasonable" behaviour, most parents can't help but wonder: was it a mistake to give in to the demand for triangle toast? But most preschoolers will gradually become more flexible as their thought processes and social skills mature.

"Control is a big issue at this age," observes Libbey. "With increasing self-awareness, children are developing control over their own behaviour, and over their lives. They are also exploring how much they can control other people's lives, so they may like to create rules for other people."

Sharon McLeod, a mother of four boys under six, observes that her three-year-old, Travis, is sometimes less concerned with following the rules himself than with ensuring that his brothers do. "He called me the other day, saying, 'Jacob's running around with food in his hand!' I said, 'So are you.' That didn't seem to have occurred to him."

Children's "invented" rules offer a fascinating glimpse of their inner thought processes. "Preschoolers create rules from their own observation, as well as what we explicitly tell them," says Libbey. Sharon recalls a conversation in which Travis announced he couldn't play with one of his preschool classmates because she was a girl. "I told him that didn't matter. So he asked if his older brothers played with girls. And I said yes, naming a little neighbour of ours as an example. And he replied, 'Well, but *she*'s not a girl!'" Once convinced there was a legitimate precedent, however, Travis decided he and Sarah could be playmates, after all.

A new awareness of rules can both enhance and complicate a preschooler's friendships. Now, and for many years to come, kids may spend as much time negotiating the "rules of the game" as actually playing ("Let's play Lion King. But I have to be Nala. No, you be Simba. I don't want any hyenas."). But sparks can fly when an overzealous child becomes bossy with her playmates. At the daycare, Libbey gently coaches children with phrases like, "You want Shelly to play it this way, but she doesn't want to do it like that. That's okay, people can like different things."

Janet notes that her five-year-old daughter, Corinne, is becoming very aware of "fairness." "She'll ask, why are the rules different for the adults, or for the baby? She wears a neck-warmer instead of a scarf because we feel it's safer on the playground, and we explained that to her. But now she's worried: shouldn't her friends wear neck-warmers, too? It's hard for her to understand that different parents might make different decisions about something like this."

Preschoolers are busy making sense of the world. But at this stage, "they don't really have the understanding yet that people can have dif-

"I'M TELLING!"

With acceptance of rules comes, very often, a concern that *everyone* follow the rules, and the emergence of a not-so-attractive behaviour: "Mrs. James, Georgia didn't put her crayons away!"

How to handle tattling? You *do*, after all, want her to speak up when something really bad is going on. What qualifies as "bad" is admittedly a grey area, one you'll be working out for years to come. But now is a good time to introduce the idea that there's a difference between "tattling" and "telling to help."

What is tattling? It's telling on another child, not to help him, or protect yourself, but to get him in trouble. That's different from telling because someone might get hurt, or something might get broken, or you need help handling a conflict. You can explore this idea with examples, in a fun way: If Georgia is playing on the road, should you tell? Yes, definitely, because she might get hurt. If Georgia is taking your toys and won't give them back when you ask her, should you tell? Yes, if you can't work things out by yourself it's okay to ask for help. If Georgia doesn't clean up her crayons, do you need to tell? No—leaving crayons out isn't dangerous. Georgia and her parents (or teacher) can work this out by themselves.

ferent approaches," explains Libbey, "They tend to see things as black or white, good or bad, right or wrong. Their thinking is not well enough developed to understand ambiguity, or to think in shades of grey."

MINE, YOURS, OURS: LEARNING TO SHARE

HERE IS A LITTLE-KNOWN LAW OF NATURE which dictates that when two siblings are placed in a room full of toys, they will both desperately and simultaneously "need" to play with Clucky the Chicken. It's the same law that governs the child who absolutely insists on giving you a bite of his spitty Fig Newton, yet seems genuinely incapable of sharing 24 crayons with a friend.

Learning to share is a rocky road for kids. Toddlers certainly have generous impulses, but their ability to share is limited by their developmental immaturity. When children near age three, however, most parents notice that their children are more able to play "with" (as opposed to "beside") other kids, and that those fierce tugs-of-war are a little less frequent.

Barb Stuart, director of the Family Studies Lab School at Guelph University, feels that children who are growing up in a healthy atmosphere will naturally develop the ability to share. "There are some developmental steps that help in learning to share," she explains. "Kids need to understand object permanence—that a toy someone has taken out of the room hasn't disappeared forever. They need to have an idea what 'belonging to' means, that your bear still belongs to you even if you let Sally play with it ... or conversely that it is still Sally's even if you've got it now. The concepts of giving things back, of taking turns ... these ideas take the anxiety out of sharing.

"There are always individual differences among children," adds Stuart. "More 'intense' kids may find it harder to share. Children experiencing extra stress in their lives will pull what they have a little closer."

The balance between respecting children's personal property and encouraging sharing is not always easy to find. In *Siblings without Rivalry*, Adele Faber and Elaine Mazlish recommend against "forced

SHARING: THE BIGGER PICTURE

Sharing, of course, is about more than toys and cookies. "It's tied up with the whole issue of civic responsibility," says Stuart. "We can expose preschoolers to the idea that we share what we have with others who are more in need." Young children understand this best, she suggests, when we use very concrete, basic, simple examples.

When you sort through outgrown clothes and baby toys together and donate them to a local thrift store, or go grocery shopping for the local food bank, this means more to a child than the cheques you may write to various charities. She doesn't understand economics, but she can imagine being hungry, or not having a warm winter coat. Talking about these things with her—at her level—will help her understand that sharing is not just a social pleasantry, but an important way of caring for others.

sharing." They argue, "*Making* children share...only makes them clutch their possessions more tightly. Forced sharing undermines goodwill."

One possible compromise is the "few precious treasures" strategy. For example, Stuart suggests that when friends are coming over to play, you might say to your child, "You know in a few minutes your friends will be arriving. They're going to want to play and have fun with your toys. If there are any very precious toys that you don't want to share, let's put them away now so no one will feel bad about them, and you can play with them after everyone has gone home." Once children are mature enough to "imagine how you would feel," they will accept this early social nicety.

Similarly, our family has a rule that toys left in the playroom are for everyone to use. If there are possessions that can't be shared, they must be put away in the owner's bedroom, not left in tantalizing view. (In a shared bedroom, this could be a special shelf, box or cupboard.) Usually, the climb upstairs is just long enough to make sharing more attractive!

The "sharing blues" with siblings seem to go on long after sharing with friends has become a way of life. By five, many children can play with their age-mates for hours in relative peace. But these same co-operative youngsters will often still resort to grabbing and yelling "Mine!" with their brothers and sisters.

Very young children who haven't yet learned the ropes pose another threat to the new sharer's composure. Watch a "civilized" four-year-old's face when a strange toddler ambles up and grabs his cracker. Chances are, he'll be outraged at this breach of etiquette. He's too close to toddlerhood himself to be able to make allowances for a baby's ignorance.

Predictable bumps in the road aside, though, Stuart feels that "if children live in a household in which sharing is valued and modelled frequently, then it will seem natural that they share, too." She also stresses that we should reinforce children's early efforts by showing our appreciation when they *do* share. (Yes, soggy cookies and all.)

You'll know the lesson is sinking in when your daughter gives little Kendra a turn on the swing: not to avoid a fight, but "because I want her to have fun."

LIFE IN THE SLOW LANE:
SLOWPOKES AND DAWDLERS
....

REAKFAST IS LONG OVER, three-year-old Allie is still in her pyjamas, and now Allie's mother, Chris McCoy, is getting a little impatient. She tells her daughter, "We've got to get dressed now!" but Allie continues dreamily playing with her toys and gives her mother a look that says, "What's the big hurry?" Finally she begins slowly sifting through the socks in her drawer, leisurely looking for just the right pair.

"Sometimes it's just like that old saying, 'the hurrieder I go, the behinder I get,'" McCoy says. "If I really start rushing her, she ends up with her shoes on the wrong feet and she's forgotten something vital and it ends up taking even longer."

Karen Leslie recalls sending her son Andrew upstairs to pick out a pair of socks and finding him twenty minutes later lying on his bed looking at a picture book. "When I asked him why he'd come upstairs, he just looked at me blankly," she says. "He really didn't remember, he'd just gotten sidetracked by other things."

Karen realizes that Andrew's dawdling isn't just procrastination to get out of something he didn't want to do, since even a walk to the park—a place Andrew loves to visit—can take forever. Andrew's always stopping, distracted by everything from puddles to bugs to dandelions. "When he stops to look at something, I'll say to him, 'Come on, we're going to the park now,' and he responds, 'Okay,' but he doesn't budge," Karen observes. "He's just so interested in the world around him."

Karen found Andrew's behaviour more frustrating, she says, when she had no other children around to compare him with. Last year she led a workshop at a La Leche League conference on "Parenting the Three-to-Five-Year-Old," and was relieved to find that many of the parents in attendance described their own children as slowpokes and dawdlers. "It helped me to discover that this is pretty normal for children in this age group," she says.

Young children have no real sense of time, she explains. They haven't the experience to accurately estimate how long ten minutes or two hours is, or the conceptual sophistication to really understand what "clock time" represents. (I remember my son Jeremy asking me to turn on *Mr. Dressup* and simply not being able to comprehend that we had missed it. He figured that *Mr. Dressup* should begin when we got back from our morning walk, even if we weren't home until lunchtime.)

Little ones also have short attention spans, and are easily distracted by anything new or potentially interesting. Yes, Andrew likes to go the park, but right now his attention is caught by the bright yellow of the dandelions in the grass that he has caught sight of en route to his destination. Leslie sees this as actually being a positive trait: "It's a plus, being able to look into a room and find lots of things to do. After all, play is the child's way of learning. It's almost as though they have to check everything out because they have so much to learn about the world."

Chris McCoy has noticed another side to Allie's dawdling—it doesn't happen when there's something she really wants to do. Allie loves the nursery school she attends three afternoons a week, and she finishes her lunch promptly and gets herself ready when McCoy tells her it's a school day.

"Sometimes I think she's just a procrastinator, like her mom," Chris says. "She tends to put things off to the last minute. But if she has a goal, like getting to school, she can move a lot faster!"

Karen also feels that being a slowpoke can be the child's way of resisting something he doesn't really want to do. (Even adults find themselves doing this!) She remembers times when, after an hour or so of trying to get Andrew ready for an outing, she's said, "Look, if we don't get ready now we can't go, we won't get there on time." Andrew's reply: "That's okay, I didn't really want to go."

SOME COMIC RELIEF

This Dennis Lee poem turns the tables on us uptight grown-ups, and lets kids get on *our* case for a change. For best effect, though, find the book and enjoy Juan Wijngaard's hilarious illustration.

> Dawdle, dawdle, dawdle,
> It's the uncles and the aunts,
> Dawdling with their shoes and socks,
> Dawdling with their pants,
>> So hurry up
>> And scurry up
>> And hurry, scurry, worry up—
> Thank goodness there are kids around
> To make them stop their dawdling.
>
> Dawdle, dawdle, dawdle
> It's the daddies and the mums,
> Dawdling with their apple juice,
> Dawdling with their crumbs.
>> So hurry up
>> And scurry up
>> And hurry, scurry, worry up—
> Thank *goodness* there are kids around
> To make them stop their dawdling!

That's fine when the outing is "optional," like a trip to the park or a visit to the library, but what about when it's a doctor's appointment or some other event that simply can't be missed? How can the parent of the slowpoke get there on time?

It helps, Chris finds, to explain the situation. "If we're just out for a walk, she likes to look at everything and we have a nature lesson along the way," says Chris. "But if we have a purpose, and I explain to her why we have to get there and when, she's quite co-operative. I try to give her a 'pot of gold at the end of the rainbow'—I explain we have to do this before you can do what you want. She usually responds quite well."

Planning ahead is key, experienced parents stress. Karen Leslie tries to start getting Andrew, his little brother Iain, and herself ready well in advance of the time they have to leave. That allows Andrew to move at his own pace. Planning around a child's daily rhythms also helps—if you know your child is slow to rev up in the morning, or becomes balky and droopy around naptime, it's wise to either build in more "getting ready" time, or schedule outings when he's peppier.

They do, eventually, outgrow this slowpoke stage. With four children, I had become accustomed to always planning well in advance—if we were going out, I started getting ready half an hour before the time I wanted to leave. One day I realized that we were arriving everywhere early. My slowpokes had grown up.

"CAN I HELP?": LETTING KIDS LEND A HAND

ET'S START WITH A COMMON-SENSE observation: no efficiency expert is going to suggest that a preschooler's help is a great way to reduce your workload. Often, it's even a little more trouble to include young children in our everyday tasks. Letting kids help isn't "efficient"—but it is valuable.

At two, Alan was regularly "helping" in the kitchen, standing beside his mom or dad on a chair and mixing cookie dough or spinning the salad. "At times it was a zoo," admits his mom, Jan Turner. "He'd be licking batter off the spoons, grabbing the eggs, dumping in extra flour. I had to keep reminding myself that the final result didn't have to be perfect. If the muffins were heavy, or the lettuce leaves nearly whole, it wasn't a big deal. Keeping it enjoyable—within the bounds of safety and reason—was more important."

Sometimes Alan's parents thought their friends, who kept their kids firmly gated out of the kitchen, might have the right idea after all. But as he grew, their early patience began to pay off. At four, Alan "invented" a recipe for cookies—with some coaching on proportions—that wasn't half bad. He could feed the dog, measuring out two cupfuls of kibble. He could even fix his own peanut butter sandwich, although the result was a little primitive.

"He sees himself as a competent person," says his father, Bob. "We let him do things with us—push the photocopy machine button, answer the phone, plant seeds in the garden, whatever—and he feels good that he knows about these things."

Child psychiatrist Joanna Santa Barbara confirms that feeling able to contribute adds to a child's sense of worth, particularly in the preschool years. "The acquisition of competence in this age-group is extraordinarily important for self-esteem."

But Santa Barbara feels there are other important reasons to encourage our child's first helping efforts: "This is how we help to shape a co-operative, compassionate human being. Children learn what we call pro-social behaviour in part by having the opportunity to be helpful, and by having their efforts valued and praised by their parents."

When Sandra Hunter organized a work party to spruce up the parent–child centre in her community, three-and-a-half-year-old Shiyana was by her side, painting the play house. Other volunteers commented on the concentration Shiyana brought to her work.

"She likes to get involved in whatever I'm doing," says Sandra, "and basically, if it's not dangerous and it doesn't really inconvenience anybody, I let her do it." Shiyana's favourite "jobs" include "supervising" the cooking, scrubbing the floor and putting the laundry into the washer.

This isn't simply indulgence; it's also early training. Sandra is a single parent who envisions a "co-operative household where everyone contributes what they can. I simply can't do everything forever." Right now, Shiyana is allowed to feel useful by helping. Later, perhaps, she'll take for granted that she's expected to pull her weight.

Santa Barbara approves of this gradual learning of responsibility. Involving children in adult tasks, she says, should not be pushed on a child who has lost interest. "If it's not fun, it's probably not worth doing." On the other hand, she suggests that even a young preschooler benefits from some age-appropriate expectations, things that are *her* job. "At two and three, for example, a child could be expected to help put away her toys. Later, she might be responsible for keeping her clothes picked up. At five, a daily job might be appropriate. These things would be seen as her contribution to the household."

Even at five, most children do better working *with* a parent on a chore than doing it alone. And anything you can do to liven up repetitive chores like picking up toys, will boost co-operation, whether it's counting different-coloured blocks as you toss them into their bin, or singing a special clean-up song as you work.

COOL KIDS' JOBS

Wouldn't it be convenient if our kids really wanted to pick up their toys and dirty clothes?

Sorry. They want to help with the "cool" jobs: painting the porch, mowing the lawn, carving the chicken....Here are some appealing jobs that little kids can handle—with you, and later on their own.

- Sorting laundry. "Whose shirt is this? Right. It goes in Daddy's pile. Whose pants?" It's slow going, but what a great "educational" activity, involving memory, classification and matching.
- Recycling. Preschoolers can carry cans and pop bottles to the blue box, and pack up the papers every week if you hold the bag. Be sure to talk to them about why we do it. They'll feel even more important knowing they're helping the environment, too.
- Spray cleaning. Fill the sprayer with something safe like a vinegar/water mixture (kids do get carried away spraying), give her a J-cloth, and point her towards the appliances, the sliding glass doors or the TV screen (*not* the guinea pig!).
- Washing dishes. Consider this "water play," and use it to keep him busy while you prepare dinner. Stand him on a chair, fill the sink with lukewarm water, some plastic cups and plates, and a few suds. Keep a bath towel on hand to mop up the floor afterwards.
- Preparing food. Your preschooler can rip up salad, put cheese and other stuff on the pizza, roll cookie dough into little balls (yum!), and husk corn. If you have time to supervise, she will love to use a real knife to cut up celery or slice the ends off the green beans.
- Loading the washing machine. Definitely requires adult supervision, but a big hit. Need to kill some time? Play "basketball" with the dirty clothes...
- Dustbusting. A hand vacuum is the ultimate child-size machine. It makes a satisfying "Vroom!" when you push the button, and the way it sucks up cracker crumbs is pretty cool, too.
- Washing the car. Preschooler heaven. But don't let her help unless you're willing to get wet!

Learning to help, says Santa Barbara, "is a very important part of the child's development. It is a gift you can give your child." But there are some cautions and guidelines to keep the experience positive.

First, don't try to involve your preschooler when a fast or perfect job is required. At times like these, suggests Santa Barbara, you can kindly say, "Thanks, but tonight is not a good time for you to help. I need to do this job quickly, by myself, this time."

Having a pint-sized helper usually means adjusting your expectations. Think of this as an activity, not a job to get through. It will probably take longer, be messier, and the result may be below your usual standards. But try not to be critical. Remember this is supposed to make your child feel good, not inadequate. While you may handle deliberate misbehaviour by temporarily dismissing your assistant, an honest mistake demands sympathy and help repairing the damage. ("Oh, oh! Milk and eggs all over the floor. Let's get a cloth and mop up together!"—and try not to grit your teeth!)

Making the work area child-friendly, suggests Santa Barbara, can make things easier on both of you. Can the lettuce be ripped up on a plastic mat on the floor? Can some clothes hooks be hung up at child-height? Maybe the bean seeds will be easier to manage if they're poured into a plastic container rather than dug out of the little packet.

And don't forget to encourage your children to help each other. Your three-year-old's efforts to comfort the new baby or draw out a shy visitor—successful or not—should be warmly appreciated.

THE SPICE OF LIFE: TALKING ABOUT DIFFERENCES

I N THE PRESCHOOL YEARS, children become aware of the many differences among people. It's an age when they ask innocent questions that mortify everyone else: "Why does that guy have a diaper pin in his ear?" or "What happened to her teeth?" It's a dicey balancing act, to try to teach our kids that while individual differences are normal and interesting, that doesn't mean we point them out in a loud voice everywhere we go!

I remember when our family's restaurant dinner was momentarily disrupted by the arrival of a new group at the next table. One elderly man spoke with the aid of a special device that allowed him to project sound following surgery on his larynx, with a rather robot-like result. Riley, who was seven, was fascinated: "Cool!" But three-year-old Jesse was frightened: he crawled into my lap, and covered his ears whenever the man spoke. Only after I took him into the lounge and explained that "the man has a problem with his throat and he needs that machine to talk to his friends" was Jesse able to return to his meal. Soon he was gleefully deciphering the man's speech: "Hey! He said *thank you!*" That was a bit embarrassing, too, but at least Jesse had understood that people who are different don't have to be scary.

How do we handle our children's curiosity—or fear—of "different" people? Christine Corke, aunt and guardian of a little girl who suffered severe facial burns, has a useful personal perspective on this question. Krystal was only one and a half when burns from scalding water required her to wear a tight facial mask for two years. "The mask just had little holes for her eyes, nostrils, mouth and ears," recalls Christine.

When Krystal came to live with the Corkes a year later, she'd had a pretty rough life. "She didn't know how to communicate or play with other children, and would back away from any approach." So Christine

GETTING TO KNOW YOU

The more familiar children become with the many differences in the world, the more comfortably they will accept and support people who differ from themselves. If your child's world tends to be rather homogeneous, you may want to make a conscious effort to broaden her horizons:

- Seek out story books and television shows which feature characters from different ethnic backgrounds and children with various disabilities. *Sesame Street*, for example, still leads the way in matter-of-fact inclusion of people of different races and abilities.
- A preschool or daycare that makes a special effort to integrate children with disabilities will give your child a valuable chance to get to know the "person beneath the handicap."
- Look for opportunities to expose your child to different "worlds" and languages: visit a market or restaurant in Chinatown, or go to a pow-wow on a nearby First Nations reserve. Be careful how you talk about what you see together, though: you're trying to convey respect for a different way of life, not exclaim at a spectacle.

was faced with the difficult task of helping Krystal become comfortable with other children, at a time when the strangeness of her mask might make it harder for her to be accepted by them.

"We started with a gym and crafts class," says Christine, "and I went with her." Christine made sure that she always took care with Krystal's clothes and hair, helping her to feel normal and pretty, and was matter-of-fact and supportive with the other children's questions.

"A lot of the kids did stare at first, and a couple were scared and cried. But the brave ones came up and asked about Krystal's mask, and I just explained it was like a special Band-Aid to help her face get better after it was hurt. I also let Krystal take off her mask, to show them that she was just a little girl with a big bandage on. It didn't take long before they didn't even notice it and welcomed Krystal's first tentative efforts to join in the play."

Christine remembers when a new girl joined the group and was frightened by Krystal's mask. "I didn't have to say anything. The other children just said, 'Oh, don't worry about it. It's just something to make her better.'"

Christine's advice for handling children's questions? "Give them a simple, matter-of-fact, reassuring explanation. Don't make them not look, or hustle them away as if it's something bad that can't be talked about. Just be normally polite, like you would to anyone."

Children can be taught quite early not to point at people or talk loudly about them, "because it might make the person feel bad or embarrassed." At the same time, we can encourage them to ask quietly about what they see, so we can either explain it right then or, if the situation seems more delicate, talk about it later.

Educators offer some other tips for talking to young children about differences. Ana Consuelo Matiella, author of *Positively Different: Creating a Bias-Free Environment for Young Children* (Network Publications, 1991), suggests that we encourage our children to see differences in a positive light, not to ignore them ("We are all the same, really") but to celebrate them ("We are all different, and that's what makes us interesting"). For example, says Matiella, a positive response to a child's question about a "funny-looking dress" might be: "The woman is wearing a sari. Women from India wear saris sometimes. Isn't the material beautiful?"

Stressing the positive isn't so easy when the difference is due to a handicap. Kathy Barnett, contributor to the book *Discover the World: Empowering Children to Value Themselves, Others and the Earth* (New Society Publishers, 1990), suggests that when talking about physical or mental limitations, "a rule to remember is 'People First.' For example, 'My friend with glasses or a student in a wheelchair.'" This helps keep the person from getting lost in a label. Barnett also suggests that we emphasize what each person *can* do, rather than dwelling on his or her limitations.

At three, Krystal Corke now confidently attends preschool, enjoys playing with the other children and is proudly mask-free. Looking back on the experience, Christine's observations are both reassuring and chilling. "The children handled it really well. It was the adults who could act very hurtfully. Some would stare to the point that Krystal got upset, and I would have to ask them to stop. They would talk about her as if she couldn't hear. One woman came up and asked, 'What does she look like under that mask?'"

As with so many things, teaching our children to be understanding of differences begins with taking a hard look at ourselves.

FUNKY FOURS: WHAT'S GOING ON?

DON'T KNOW WHAT'S GOT INTO CAREY these days," my neighbour said, sighing. "He used to be so co-operative, so eager to please, so happy. But suddenly he's driving us nuts. He's clingy and defiant. He has these big tantrums when he doesn't get his way. Frankly, I'm worried about him."

"Didn't Carey turn four a few months ago?" I asked.

"Yes, why?"

"Four can be a tough age. Everyone's prepared for the 'terrible twos,' but nobody tells you about four," I said. "He may just have hit a 'rough patch' in his development."

Children don't develop in a smooth, ascending line. Instead, they tend to forge ahead, and then fall back, in a sort of spiral pattern. Frances Ilg and Louise Bates Ames, co-founders of the Gesell Institute of Human Development, have documented this pattern quite carefully. In their book *Child Behavior*, they characterize four-year-olds with the key words "out of bounds."

As Joanne Tee, a family counsellor in Hamilton, Ontario, explains, "Threes tend to be more placid and settled, but four is an age of more turmoil. They're just smart enough at four to question the things you say, to worry more about what might happen, to protest when something 'isn't fair.'"

Lisa Morrison, mother of four-year-old Ariel, sees this as a challenging age when growing independence is matched with new verbal skills. "I can ask my daughter to do something, and she has tons of reasons why not. She has started to question everything I say, things she used to just accept."

Lisa is able to see that argumentativeness (or defiance!) as a positive sign of her daughter's blossoming intelligence. "I can see her thinking about things, trying to understand the world. Sometimes I'll tell her

FOUR GOING ON TEN? THE PRESCHOOLER WITH OLDER SIBLINGS
Four is a bit of a high-pressure year, anyway, for many children, but the ups and downs can be even more pronounced when there are older siblings in the picture.

At best, an older sibling is a friend, protector, and guide to the world of "big kids." Many childhood rites of passage, like starting kindergarten, are easier for younger siblings: when you've been visiting your big sister's classroom for three years, and recognize her friends on the playground or on the bus, school is a much more familiar environment. And younger siblings often have an enviable comfort level with other kids of all ages.

But the pressure to "keep up" can be intense. While other four-year-olds are delighted if they manage to stay upright on skates, she may be comparing herself to a figure-skating big sister. And while his little classmates are content just to cheer on Luke Skywalker, he may be desperately trying to match a ten-year-old brother's encyclopaedic knowledge of every *Star Wars* character, location and technical specification.

The bottom line? Older siblings are exciting and stimulating, but they can also be demanding and exhausting. If your preschooler is acting "stressed out," it might be worth making sure he's getting enough time and space to be the little kid he really is, away from older children's judgements. A quiet afternoon just with you, making cookies and singing along to a children's tape, or a playdate at a friend's house, can give him a much-needed respite. (You might also want to ask big brother and sister—privately—to ease up on their expectations.)

something and days later she'll come back and ask me a question about it, and I know she's been analysing what I said—thinking it over. It's amazing."

But for some fours, that greater thoughtfulness can go hand in hand with greater feelings of anxiety and caution.

Hannah Bailey says that both her sons (now ages eight and 11) were less independent at age four than they had been at three. "It was as though they took a step backwards. They were more clingy and less confident." She even remembers her children developing nervous habits—sucking on a finger, for example, or chewing fingernails. "They were just emotionally more volatile and more stressed."

Her son Rhys, for example, was invited to a birthday party at a neighbour's when he was four—a neighbour he'd visited many times. Rhys wanted to go, but he wanted his mom to come too. When she explained that she couldn't stay long because she had errands to run, he burst into tears. "At three," Hannah says, "he would have gone off to that party quite happily."

Pretty typical, according to Tee. "Remember how your toddler would walk away and explore the world, then climb back on your lap to regroup for a little while before taking those next steps away from you? The same kind of thing happens to many children at four—a time of clinging before becoming a more independent five."

Another facet of your four-year-old, says Tee, is a high energy level that he can't always keep under control. That's why some of these kids can seem surprisingly forceful. Scarlet Vertolli, mother of four-year-old Dillon, says, "If Dillon wants something, he's going to get it. He can be quite aggressive, and sometimes it's hard to know how to handle that."

Gently, according to Tee. "Be careful you don't get into labelling the child as an aggressive kid just because he doesn't always control himself. Children this age may also 'lie' and 'steal'—but these are adult labels." And while you probably want to teach your child that honesty is the best policy, it's important to remember that for your four-year-old, there are lots of grey areas when it comes to truth. Sometimes a preschooler's idea of a joke, for example, can be to really get you going with a tall tale, but that doesn't mean he's lying in the adult sense.

Many children make their school debuts with junior kindergarten around this age, too, and while they will often enjoy school, it can be pretty hard on them. The stress of being "good" all day for teachers can be tough on an energetic little person. Morrison says, "At nursery school, they say Ariel is an angel, and she's always very co-operative at other people's homes. I try to keep in mind that being on her best behaviour at school probably isn't always easy for her."

Sometimes your four-year-old may seem like a walking, talking mass of contradictions. One minute he's clinging and cautious, the next he's bursting with independence and confidence. He plunges from giddy, abandoned laughter to equally abandoned anger (or tears) with dizzying speed. As Debbie McGill, mother of four-year-old Stephanie, says: "I think when you have your first child, four seems very grown-up, but they're not really. They still need a lot of attention and nurturing, even when they're being challenging and defiant.

"You need some new skills to be the parent of a four-year-old," says Morrison. "You need to parent in a conscious way, to be thinking about what you're doing and saying. A four-year-old won't accept 'because I said so.'" And chances are she'll make a point of reminding you that "'because' is not a reason!"

READY FOR PRESCHOOL?: STARTING NURSERY SCHOOL OR KINDERGARTEN

 HEN SUE AUSTIN DECIDED TO SEND her three-year-old son, Graham, to nursery school, she had many hopes for the program, but early academics were not among them. "I don't think nursery school should be about academics," she emphasizes. "These are *little* kids. They need their childhood." Instead, Sue wanted to give Graham a chance to "broaden his horizons. I wanted him to be comfortable with other children and adults, to learn to enjoy relationships with others. I thought it would be a gentle introduction to a new environment, new activities, and time spent away from me."

Graham enjoyed his year at nursery school, and the following year Sue discovered another bonus: "It was a good stepping stone to kindergarten," she reflects. "There are more staff at a nursery school, and it's easier for them to ease a child in. When Graham got to kindergarten, with a bigger class in a big school, he could think to himself, 'I've been through this routine before.'"

Nursery school and, where it's available, junior kindergarten (see sidebar, p. 31), can be an enriching experience for many children. But not every child is ready for a group program at three, or even four.

Susan Strachan's three-year-old son T.J. is, as she says, "a bundle of questions." He's very verbal, very energetic and eager to discover the world. Not surprisingly, Susan is considering sending him to preschool. "I'm beginning to wonder if school would help to answer his questions and encourage him to spread his wings a bit further. But how do you know when your child is ready?"

Often it seems that the timing of preschool entrance is determined entirely by a child's age, but educators and other professionals who work with kids point out how important it is to consider the individual development of each child. In her booklet *Your Child: From 3½ to 4½*, child

30

PRESCHOOL PROGRAMS: WHAT'S IN A NAME?
Nursery school or kindergarten—what's the difference? Read on.

- **Nursery school:** Nursery schools charge fees, and follow similar staff-to-child ratios as licensed daycare. Most are geared to three- and four-year-olds, though some accommodate a wider age range. In a good nursery school, most staff have ECE (Early Childhood Education) training. Programs are usually half-day, often just two or three days a week.

- **Junior kindergarten:** Where available, junior kindergarten is funded by the Ministry of Education, located in elementary schools, and staffed by elementary teachers. It's not offered in every province, though, or by every school board in provinces where it's an option. While specific birth-date regulations vary provincially, this is a program geared to four-year-olds. Programs are usually half-time (either half-days or, particularly since the advent of widespread funding cuts, alternate full days). Staff-to-child ratios are considerably lower than for licensed childcare and nursery schools, and classes may be bigger, so the children need to be a little more independent.

- **Senior kindergarten:** The same thing, but for five-year-olds, and with more emphasis on "pre-math" and "pre-reading" skills. Some schools have split classes combining junior and senior kindergarten, and these can work out very well (the older kids who know the ropes help the new kids settle in). Like JK, senior kindergarten is an optional program, even though it's part of the school system.

psychologist Sarah Landy, of the C.M. Hincks Institute in Toronto, gives parents some useful advice. She points out that it's better to have your two-, three- or four-year-old start school a little later and succeed, than to start him too early, when he might experience failure or frustration. The former will help build his self-esteem, while the latter might erode it.

What are some signs of readiness for preschool? It depends to a certain extent on the individual program: some nursery schools are geared to children as young as two; many are also well-equipped to meet the needs of children with speech or motor difficulties. Other programs may be more demanding, requiring children to have independent toilet skills, for example, or expecting children to have mastered early academic abilities like counting, sorting and letter recognition.

In any program, though, a child needs to be able to cope with a group of other children, adapt to a new set of routines and rules, and separate (perhaps after a settling-in period) from her parents or caregiver.

In T.J.'s case, while Susan felt that he would enjoy the activities a preschool program might offer, she worried about how he would handle the emotional challenges, like the separation from her. "T.J. very much wants to be with me. He likes to be around other kids, but he really wants me to be there as well. I worried that he wouldn't be happy at school without me."

For parents of children in daycare, there may be other considerations, too. Sending a child to nursery school or junior kindergarten may complicate childcare arrangements, since many programs are only part-time and therefore require transportation and daycare for the rest of the day. And for a child who doesn't handle changes well, adding a transition to preschool on top of the daily trek to daycare may be just too stressful.

On the other hand, while a good daycare centre will already include an early childhood education program, nursery school or kindergarten can add enrichment to informal daycare. And if all the four-year-olds in your daughter's daycare are heading off to JK in the fall, your daughter will probably want to go too, especially if she is very sociable and eager for new experiences.

Most preschool programs hold registration in the spring. If you're interested in enrolling your child, phone schools in your area and ask if they would welcome a visit. Talk to the teachers, and watch how they interact with the children. Find out what their program goals are, and what happens over the course of the day. Ask a few of the parents what they like about the school. And if you have special concerns about your child's readiness, talk them over with the staff.

HOW ABOUT LESSONS?

When Lynn Moffat's son, Iain, was four, she enrolled him in a pottery class for preschoolers. But Iain's participation didn't make it to the end of the second lesson. What went wrong?

"The teacher didn't really want me to stay, but every time I started to leave the room, Iain would fall apart," recalls Lynn. Ian didn't like the structured approach of the class, either. "What pottery meant to Iain was messing around with clay and making things out of it. That turned out to be only a small part of the program. He's happier just playing with clay at home and figuring out for himself what he can do with it."

While lessons can be appealing to some young children, it's important that they be geared to the interests and needs of a preschooler. Look for:

- A low teacher–child ratio. Preschoolers need hands-on help, and plenty of it.
- An emphasis on fun, not competition and drill. In a preschool gymnastics class, for example, children should start learning basic skills mostly through play activities (like following obstacle courses on gymnastics equipment and tumbling mats), not through repeated forward-roll drills.
- Flexibility about the parent's presence. Not all preschoolers can confidently leave their parents, and sensitive instructors understand this.
- A balance of structure and open-endedness. Obviously, you can't let a group of non-swimmers have free play in the pool! But in general, a lot of verbal instruction and rigid directions are not for preschoolers. There should be lots of hands-on experience and a chance to "do their own thing."

Sue Austin chose her son's nursery school mainly because she was so impressed by the staff. "Graham's teachers were wonderful," she enthuses. "They really looked out for the children's emotional well-being, and they welcomed the parents at any time. It was a good experience for all of us."

Susan Strachan's final decision? She put off formal preschool for a year and found a weekly library program for T.J. instead. He spends the time with his group in one room while she waits with other parents in the main library—an arrangement that helps T.J. feel comfortable about mom being close by, and yet gives him some independent social and learning experiences.

Whether you opt for early, later, or no preschool, be prepared to re-evaluate your arrangements if, after a reasonable trial period, your child seems persistently unhappy. As Liz Goldsworthy, mother of two boys (one of whom started preschool at age three, the other at five), reminds us, "Your decision is not cast in stone. There are always alternatives. If one thing isn't working—you enrolled your child in school and he's miserable, or you decided to keep your child at home and she's pining for her friends in school—then it's time to try something else."

Back to Basics:
Eating, Sleeping, Peeing

Adrienne Leong

NOT AGAIN! OR RATHER, STILL! Did you think you'd be through with these issues by now? A lucky few are. If that's you, go ahead and skip the section. But if your preschooler is still in diapers, or fights his bedtime every night, or wants nothing but French fries and waffles to eat, take comfort: many other parents are troubled by the same concerns. Basic body maintenance continues to play a big role in the parent–child relationship.

One of the reasons these issues are unsettling to parents is that they highlight the limits of our power. To rephrase an old saying, you can lead a child to bed, but you can't make her sleep! Similarly, as a parent you are responsible for giving your child a nutritious diet, to help her stay healthy. But can—or should—you "make" her eat it? Constant conflict over food makes mealtimes a trial for everyone, and hardly encourages positive attitudes towards food. What's a parent to do? We have to learn to balance our children's need for guidance and limits with their need for independence.

The good news is that, as kids grow up, many of our worries about these physical basics tend to disappear by themselves. As your child matures, his appetite, sleep habits and toileting skills will follow suit. Sometimes it just takes a little patience.

NIGHT NIGHT, SLEEP TIGHT:
ROUTINES FOR A PEACEFUL BEDTIME

 HE TITLE OF ONE OF MERCER MAYER'S popular "Little Critter" books is *Just Go To Bed!* (Western Publishing, 1988). And what parent hasn't wished at the end of a long and tiring day that their preschooler would quietly do just that?

It rarely happens that way. Most preschoolers need some help in making the transition from waking to sleeping. A good bedtime routine can help with that transition by providing three important things: a warning that bedtime is coming up, a time of closeness that eases the separation of sleeping, and a way to help the child relax and feel secure so he or she can sleep.

Jean Andrews, mother of three-year-old Hazen, describes a bedtime routine that works well for them.

Each evening at around seven, Hazen has a bath and then a story. ("He especially likes the story—he's a real book-lover," Jean adds.) He drinks a glass of milk, brushes his teeth, and then Jean takes an envelope, draws a heart on it and writes his name (Hazen calls this his "letter"), and puts it under his favourite doll. She may cuddle him a little in bed, then puts on his music box to play "Old MacDonald" and leaves him to fall asleep alone.

"If we forget anything, he calls us back," Jean says. "He has to have his milk, and the letter has to be there, or we have to go back. But generally he falls asleep by eight."

Jean says she's "pretty strict about bedtime" and has been since Hazen was an infant, emphasizing that she wanted him to learn to fall asleep alone at an early age.

Adele Hollingsworth, the mother of Thomas, six, and Josh, four, takes a different approach. The bedtime routine for her boys is fairly flexible.

LITTLE NIGHT OWLS
Just like adults, some children are at their best in the morning, while others tend to "come alive" in the evening. If your preschooler is a night owl, an early evening bedtime may not be realistic. These tips may help you accommodate each other:

- Try to limit late-afternoon naps. A night owl who has already had a long afternoon sleep may still be going strong well past *your* bedtime. If your child is not ready to give up napping altogether, try to help her sleep as early in the day as possible, and wake her up after an hour or so.
- Help her "wind down" on her own. It isn't fair (or possible) to force her to sleep when she's not ready, but she might be able to play quietly in her room until she feels tired. If you feel the need for some "grown-up time" in the evening, this can be a good compromise. A music or story tape can be a relaxing end to the day, as well. When she's older, this routine will naturally extend to reading or listening to the radio in bed. You can pop in to give her a kiss and cuddle goodnight at lights-out time.
- De-stress mornings. Many "night personalities" take a while to rev up in the morning. Try to avoid rushing your night owl when he wakes up—if you have to be somewhere at a certain time, get him up a little earlier and plan things like what to wear the night before.

"In the summer, if the weather is good, they may play outside until it starts to get dark. Then they're tired and we don't bother with much of a routine. If they're inside all evening, we usually read several stories—we may be reading for an hour or more."

Usually the boys have a bath, too, either before or after story time, and then they get ready for bed.

"I almost always give them what they call a 'start–off'—that just means I lie down with them until they fall asleep," says Adele.

The boys share a room with a trundle bed, with Thomas sleeping in the top bed and Josh in the pull-out lower bed. Adele usually lies down beside Josh, after giving Thomas a hug and kiss. She finds they generally fall asleep quite quickly, and thinks her presence helps relax them.

Some lucky parents find that bedtime can be relaxing for them, too. "My four-year-old actually likes bedtime," claims Richard Pavic. "With two older siblings, it's the one time of the day she can be sure of a parent's undivided attention! We cuddle in bed and read, the dog curls up by her feet, after lights out we chat a bit. It's not always so idyllic, but often it's a really nice, peaceful time. Sometimes *I* fall asleep!"

Sheila Stubbs, whose four children range from eight years to seven months, jokes, "My kids are allergic to bedtime." She tried a number of different bedtime routines before finding one that works well for her family.

"I used to read stories to them every night, but it was out of a sense of duty, not because I enjoyed it, and it got harder and harder as we had more kids," she remembers. She also found that some other bedtime "rituals," like giving drinks, mostly just took up a lot of time without helping the kids get to sleep.

The change that Sheila says helped the most was putting all three of the older children in a room together. They hated sleeping alone in separate rooms, Sheila discovered, and letting them share a room made bedtime much easier.

She also eliminated the stories and other parts of the routine that weren't working. "Now I just give them a warning: get your pyjamas on, have a drink or snack if you want it, go to the bathroom, because it's bedtime in 15 minutes. When the time arrives, I take them up to bed, give hugs and kisses, and that's it. They usually talk together for a while, and then they fall asleep."

Sheila also suggests not worrying too much about a set bedtime until the children are old enough to be getting up for school.

"If it works better in your family to have the children up until ten or eleven at night, go ahead and do it. They can sleep in the next morning.

AFRAID OF THE DARK?
Preschoolers are an imaginative bunch, and nighttime fears are common.
For some children, it's that dark room that triggers scary fantasies about
monsters or ghosts. If your child is scared of the dark, you might take com-
fort in parent educator Kathy Lynn's assurance: "There are no support
groups that I know of for adult survivors of sleeping with the light on in
childhood!"
   Remember, kids don't necessarily have the same sleep associations that
we do. *You* might need a darkened room to fall asleep, but if your child
feels better with a light on, it's unlikely to keep her awake. We know of one
family where all three children sleep—soundly—with their overhead lights
blazing. But a low-wattage table lamp or even a night light may be all your
child needs to feel brave again.

Or if you're working, you may want to spend the evening with your child and let her take a long nap at the babysitter's in the afternoon. There's no universal law that says preschoolers should be in bed by 7:30."

The ideal bedtime routine is the one that works best for your child and family. Some children need a longer winding-down period than others, and some parents are happy to stay with their children until they fall asleep, while others prefer not to. If your current bedtime plan isn't working, remember that the traditional bath-and-story routine isn't carved in stone, and try a change.

"CAN I SLEEP WITH YOU?": HOW TO HANDLE LATE-NIGHT VISITORS

HREE A.M. You're startled out of sleep by the sound of pattering feet, moving quickly: thump, thump, thump, thump, *thump!* A small body clutching a large pillow appears by your bedside. "I had a bad dream," Rachel says between sniffles. "Can I come in?"

Yes, no, maybe so—parents' responses to night visits from their preschoolers depend on two main factors: (1) whether they're comfortable with the *idea* of a child in their bed, and (2) whether they can actually get any sleep with a child in their bed.

"I don't know how people can sleep with their kids," confesses Debbie Fisico, mother of three young boys ages two, five and seven. "Maybe my kids are more active or something, but I can't take it!"

Debbie and her husband, Carmen, are happy to have their kids pile in for an early-morning visit, but they also like having one place (i.e., the bedroom) where they can usually count on being alone. If a child wakes up at night (which happens seldom with the two older boys), Debbie or Carmen will comfort him in his own room.

Wendy and Gaston Dozois have four children ranging in age from two to 11, and they've spent lots of time with small visitors in their bed. "We have a queen-size bed," says Wendy. "That's key. You couldn't do it with a double."

"Our kids all had really different sleep patterns," Wendy observes. "Jamie, our oldest, had colic as a baby and woke up frequently in the first year. For a couple of years after that he'd wake up and come in with us maybe half the time. Sometimes one of us would lie down with him in his bed instead, but it was usually easiest to just let him climb in."

Jamie gradually woke up less and less, but continued to "trail into our room" occasionally until he was six or seven. "By then it was get-

NIGHTMARES AND NIGHT TERRORS

Preschoolers, with their active imaginations and still-fledgling grasp of the boundaries between real and pretend, can be quite susceptible to scary dreams and nightmares. And whatever your normal rules about who sleeps where, most experts and parents agree that when a child is sobbing from terrifying dream, she needs comforting right away. Usually, that's *all* she needs. Yes, you can monster-proof the windows and check under the bed, but probably just staying with her (in your room or hers) until your reassuring presence allows her to drift back off to sleep will do the trick.

Night terrors are less common, thankfully, because they're a lot harder on parents. Typically, you'll find your child with his eyes open, thrashing and screaming wildly. You try to comfort him and he doesn't even seem to know you're there—or he may even shrink back from you in horror. In fact, he is not fully awake and your only recourse is to wait for him to sink back into sleep on his own (which may happen quite suddenly), or try to get through enough to wake him up. It's pointless to try to reason with him, but your soothing voice or touch may help (though very often nothing seems to help). If he does wake up, just calmly help him back to sleep. He probably won't even remember what happened.

If your child suffers frequent nightmares or night terrors you might want to take a look at her daytime life. Overtiredness, high anxiety or stress, and, yes, too-scary videos can be contributing factors. Older preschoolers may find some relief in talking about their nightmares, and especially in "rewriting" the endings ("What do you wish had happened instead? You could imagine that dragon flying away when you clapped your hands, or even making friends and taking you for a ride!").

ting crowded," Wendy says, and laughs; "so we told him he had to sleep on the floor if he wanted to come in."

Wendy's second baby, Jonathon, proved to be "a wonderful sleeper" who always preferred his own bed to his parents'. Kimberly (now four) has also stayed in her own bed most of the time. Two-year-old Matthew, however, seems to be following in his oldest brother's footsteps. He sleeps so much better in his parents' bed than in his crib, explains

Wendy, that "right now he sleeps with us most of the time."

How do Wendy and Gaston feel about their nighttime company? "I'm used to it," says Wendy, "Everyone gets back to sleep faster than if we try to keep everyone in their own beds. Gaston is a light sleeper, but he says he really doesn't mind having the kids in bed—it bothers him worse to hear them calling or crying at night.

"There is some loss of privacy," acknowledges Wendy, "but we still manage to find time alone together."

An "open-door" bed works very well for some families—but it isn't for everyone. "We like snuggling with our kids, but we don't want to end up with a family bed," explains Greg Sheffield. "We have friends whose seven-year-old still sleeps with them, and we don't want to encourage that habit." When Greg and Lucy's three-year-old began visiting at night, after moving to a big bed, they were sympathetic ("It's hard to explain why Mom and Dad get to sleep together, and he can't," says Lucy). But unless it's nearly morning, Greg usually takes Justin back to his own bed and helps him back to sleep there.

If you, too, would rather have your bed to yourself, and your preschooler is bent on joining you, there are alternatives that still show your child that you're there for her if she needs you at night. But your child's individual temperament and sleep style will have a lot to do with how easily she accepts the substitutes you offer. Some strategies other parents have tried:

Sit or lie down with the child in *his* bed until he's asleep. "It takes me a long time to get back to sleep anyway," says father Bill Currie, "and this is a nice, quiet time together. Then I can go back to my own bed and sleep without little toes digging in my ribs."

Put a small foam mattress and sleeping bag on the floor beside your bed, and tell the child she can quietly snuggle in there if she needs to be near you.

Offer an incentive. This works only with a child old enough to understand a delayed reward, and who is really ready to sleep alone (that is, he comes in because it's a pleasant habit, not out of any real fear or discomfort). It goes something like this, "You know, Ian, Daddy and I don't sleep very well when you're in bed with us, and we think you're big enough to stay in your own bed now. To help you learn, we'll give you a star every time you stay in your bed all night." Depending on the child's age and preferences, the star might earn an immediate reward the next morning, or be saved up for a bigger reward (e.g., a small toy for seven stars). It's best, though, not to demand a certain number of nights *in a row* for the reward; that's very stressful for a child who has a scary dream on the sixth night!

Find some other company for the child. Wendy's Jamie woke up much less at night once he began to share a double bed with his younger brother. "I think Jamie just didn't like being alone," muses Wendy. Marianne Drew-Pennington's daughter, Elizabeth, resisted all attempts to dissuade her from climbing in with her mother until, at age nine, she got a kitten. "The kitten sleeps in her room and she won't leave because she thinks the kitten might be lonely," marvels Marianne. (But don't acquire a pet solely for this purpose; it may just as easily *cause* night disturbances!)

Boost the child's "security quotient." Marianne observes that increased night waking/visiting can accompany new fears or stresses in a child's life. Extra time and cuddles with your child, a bedtime routine that is soothing and predictable, and maybe talking during the day about any changes or worries she may be coping with (a new baby, a sick grandparent?) may contribute to more peaceful sleep.

And if nothing works? Some families have gone so far as to put their bed frame in storage and just lay down two mattresses side by side in the master bedroom. Or maybe you'd rather sleep on the couch ...

STILL IN DIAPERS?: DELAYED TOILET TRAINING

UR IDEAS ABOUT WHEN CHILDREN should graduate from diapers to using the toilet have changed quite dramatically since the beginning of this century. Today many people feel that too-early toilet training can cause problems, and parents watch their children for signs of readiness rather than watching the calendar.

Signs of readiness to use the toilet include:

- going for several hours with dry diapers
- understanding that dry pants are preferable
- understanding the connection between using the potty and keeping her pants dry
- recognizing the sensations of a full bladder and the need to have a bowel movement
- having the ability to (at least briefly) delay the urge to go to the bathroom long enough to get there.

These signs do not appear in most cases until after the child is two or two and a half, but waiting usually pays off in a quicker, easier learning process. Sometimes, though, a child passes age three, or even four, without giving up diapers, and then parents may become concerned. Why isn't he using the toilet like the other kids do?

Shauna Mackenzie's three daughters were all "trained" at about age three. Once summer arrived, Shauna simply let them run around their rural property without diapers, and they quickly learned to use the toilet.

But this approach did not work with her son, Peter. After a summer of freedom, Peter insisted on returning to full-time diapers in the fall and would plug his ears whenever Shauna tried to bring up the topic of

WHEN THERE'S A PROBLEM

It's important for parents to be aware that a variety of medical problems, from urinary tract infection to congenital malformations, can sometimes cause delayed toilet readiness.

Marilyn Willows remembers her daughter Diane running around without a diaper at age one. "She'd leave a trail of drops behind her all the time," Marilyn says. As Diane grew, toilet training was impossible. Marilyn was advised, "She'll grow out of it," but was unconvinced. She began keeping a diary of Diane's wetting patterns that revealed an almost constant dribble of urine. With that as a guide, the doctor was able to diagnose a rare congenital condition that was helped by surgery.

If you have any concerns that your child's delayed toilet training may be related to a physical (or emotional) problem, check it out with your child's doctor. A diary like Marilyn's, identifying any unusual patterns or behaviours, can be very helpful.

using the toilet. "I decided not to worry about it since he'd only just turned three," Shauna says. "I expected he'd learn next summer."

By the next summer, though, Peter refused to even consider using the toilet. "Every couple of months I would ask him why he didn't want to use the toilet, and he couldn't answer me," Shauna remembers. "I didn't want to pressure him. Sometimes his sisters or his cousins tried to encourage him—they'd take him in with them when they used the toilet. But it didn't make any difference."

Shauna was confident that Peter had no physical problems because his diapers were often dry for many hours. She noticed, though, that wet or messy diapers didn't bother him at all and he rarely asked to have them changed. So she waited.

The summer Peter turned five, Shauna decided to give him a nudge towards using the toilet. She used up the rest of the disposable diapers on hand, and didn't buy any more.

"Peter had taken off his wet diaper when he woke up, and asked for a new diaper, and I told him they were all gone. We checked the cupboard to be certain. Peter went back and continued playing Lego with his sister. I could see him beginning to squirm and look uncomfortable, but I didn't say anything. He came over and asked me if I could go and buy him some diapers, and I said I was busy just now but maybe I could go in the afternoon. About half an hour later he ran into the bathroom and shut the door. I heard a flush and then he was back playing Lego with his sister again."

Peter never asked for a diaper again and never had an accident. Shauna says that for the first two weeks he was reluctant to leave the house for long in case he had to use a strange bathroom, but he soon was happy using any toilet.

Shauna's pleased that toilet training never became a battle of wills. "It's hard to wait when other children are doing it much earlier. It helped

---

BEDWETTING

For many children, dry nights quickly follow dry days. But a significant number—15 percent of five-year-olds, the majority of them boys—will continue to wet the bed long after daytime toilet training has been mastered.

What to do? For the time being, patience and "pull-ups" or a good waterproof bed pad are your best bet. "In most cases, this is simply a matter of slower-than-average development," explains urologist John Hambley.

Bedwetting is out of the child's control (he can't *make* himself wake up or "hold it"), and seems to be at least partly hereditary. So it is pointless at best, and cruel at worst, to punish, scold or belittle a child who wets the bed. The more matter-of-fact you can be, the better.

The good news is that in the vast majority of cases, the problem *will* resolve itself. Without any treatment at all, the 15 percent at age five will decline to 1 percent by age 15. But if, sometime after age six, your child becomes upset by her bedwetting and wants to give Nature a nudge, there are training programs that can help older children work towards dry nights. Ask your doctor.

---

me to know of a few other children who were four or five before they used the toilet. If the average age is two and a half or three, there will always be some who are much earlier and some who are much later."

As in so many other areas of development, children learn to use the toilet at different ages. While toilet training past age three or four can, in some cases, be a symptom of a physical or psychological problem (see "When there's a problem"), it is often just a normal variation in development.

THE GOOD, THE BAD AND THE YUCKY: THE PICKY EATER

....

SOMETIMES I THINK MY KIDS have survived the preschool period on breakfast cereal!" quips father of two William Gunter. "Seriously, my five-year-old, Meredith, tends to be hungry in the morning and will often eat a major bowl of cereal. That gets some whole grain and milk into her, which is a pretty good start. And she usually isn't very interested in dinner, but she'll shovel down another bowl of cereal before bed. It's not all she eats, of course, but it's sort of an anchor in her diet."

Quirky eating habits are endemic at this age, and it worries parents on two counts. First, we naturally wonder whether the child who refuses many foods is getting adequate nutrition; and second, we're not sure, in the long term, how best to encourage the healthy food attitudes we want our children to grow up with. Should we push them to try foods they dislike? Or should we accept their food preferences, unreasonable as they may seem?

Nathalie Béland, a dietitian in the Failure to Thrive and Feeding Disorder Clinic at Montreal Children's Hospital, points out that food dislikes are not only very common in the preschool years, but bewilderingly fickle: "Most picky eaters don't like something this week but another week it might be something else. These likes and dislikes are mostly temporary and transient. If a child chronically doesn't eat a particular food, this is his natural preference, and as long as he eats from all the food groups this isn't a problem. My advice is to offer a good variety and leave the child the option to eat what he wants."

But if he eats what he wants, will he get what he needs? Author and paediatrician T. Berry Brazelton points out, in his book *Touchpoints*, that children actually need less than many parents think: "For a finicky eater, the basic minimum diet is not very elaborate: sixteen ounces of

"I'M NOT HUNGRY"

Even if a child eats a reasonable variety of food, his parents may wonder whether he's eating "enough." But health professionals advise that the best judge of "enough" is usually the child himself.

"You control the *quality* of food children eat, not the *quantity*," suggests dietitian Nathalie Béland. "The quantity of food a child needs depends greatly on the individual. You can't compare what one child eats to what his brother ate at the same age. And the amount varies in time—a child may eat more one week, less another week."

Having said that, Béland does have some suggestions for the child who is rarely hungry at mealtime:

- **Time snacks more carefully.** "One mistake we often make is to give snacks that are too big, and too close to meals," says Béland. "If a child who has a small appetite to begin with has a snack an hour before mealtime, she won't feel like eating again. Also, drinks fill children up. If you have a child who isn't eating, look at the quantity of liquids she's taking in, especially before the meal."

- **Give small servings.** Parents who are concerned about their child's appetite may give generous servings at meals, hoping more will get eaten. More often, though, that big mound of food on the plate discourages the child. "If a child is a problem eater," says Béland, "give half the usual serving size. If she finishes it, then offer more."

- **Look at her health, not her plate.** If your child is growing to your doctor's satisfaction, shows no signs of malnutrition, and eats with gusto when she *is* hungry, you can trust that she's not starving herself.

We are born with a body that tells us when it needs food, and when it is full. We override that mechanism at our peril: chances are you know at least one adult whose eating patterns seem completely estranged from his or her natural hunger signals. Children can, and do, become engrossed in play and forget to eat, or become too upset to eat, or feel too tired to eat. So they sometimes need adult guidance in the food department. But that guidance is best geared towards helping them tune in to their *own* appetite.

THE GOOD, THE BAD AND THE YUCKY

milk, two ounces of protein, some whole-grain bread or cereal, a few ounces of fruit, and a multivitamin. The latter is needed only if she is not eating well." (And in fact many health professionals would argue that the vitamin is rarely required; most "picky eaters" do, in fact, over the course of a few days, enjoy a reasonably varied diet.)

"Right now, Francis (age three), isn't too big on dinner. He likes shepherd's pie and macaroni and cheese, and not much else," observes his mother, Diane Lee. "He does like vegetables, though." William is a bit envious of this: Meredith, he reports, "would be happy to be a vegetarian—*without* the vegetables!" However, since Meredith happily eats cheese, peanut butter and "almost any fruit," William figures she's compensating fairly well for her low intake of meat and veggies.

Béland points out that snacks can be used to fill in the nutritional gaps in a child's diet. "You don't want to make a big deal out of eating issues, or turn mealtime into a struggle," she advises. "If a child didn't have any milk for lunch, you might give him yogurt or ice cream for a snack, or he might prefer veggies and dip in the afternoon to cooked carrots at dinner." (We discuss snacks in more detail in the next chapter.)

This brings up the issue, though, of how much parents should "cater" to their child's food dislikes. If you accept her food refusals, and even offer alternatives, aren't you encouraging her to become even more "picky"?

Most health professionals feel that it's best not to get into a power struggle about food. "Fussy eaters don't dislike foods on purpose. They don't enjoy not liking something," explains Béland. "If meals become a struggle, it can develop into a personal conflict as the child tries to control what she eats, and if you try to force feed her, then she may refuse to eat more things, and this can really start to affect your relationship with your child." When meals become a source of anxiety and tension, rather than a shared family pleasure, children's attitudes towards food can become very negative.

EATING DISORDERS IN PRESCHOOLERS

Is a small appetite or picky eating *ever* a health concern? Yes, occasionally.

"There are some children who, from birth, are poor eaters or have little interest or drive to eat. Others have poor feeding skills—they may have difficulty chewing, or gag easily on foods with textures, or take an extremely long time to eat," explains Montreal dietitian Nathalie Béland. "If they are truly eating too little, or missing important types of food, their growth may be compromised."

If you are concerned that your child may eat so little or so poorly that her growth or health is at risk, it's worth checking out your concerns with your child's doctor, and perhaps a dietitian as well.

Instead, there are positive ways to encourage more adventurous eating, and maintain reasonable expectations about food:

Offer simple alternatives to disliked foods, but don't prepare elaborate "kids' meals" (except for special occasions). Nothing triggers a nasty food conflict like the child who refuses to eat the dish you've prepared especially for her. But it takes little effort to put out a plate of raw carrots and cheese cubes, in addition to the family's stew.

Eat well yourself. During family meals, let your kids see how *you* enjoy a variety of foods. Foster the assumption that, as kids grow up, their taste buds do, too.

Applaud, but don't demand, tasting. A preschooler who tries a new food is showing a certain amount of courage. If she takes a cautious sip of clam chowder, and then says "Yuck!" casual praise is still in order. "Don't like it? It's good that you tried it, though. Sometimes new foods are really yummy."

Keep offering disliked foods now and then. After all, he'll never work up the nerve to try asparagus if he never sees it again!

Experiment with different presentations. Does your child tend to be hungrier at lunch than dinner? If he's iffy on vegetables, he might eat them more readily at lunch. Or he may prefer his cereal dry, with a glass of milk on the side, rather than "all wet." We know one little boy who didn't like chicken, until he tried dipping a piece in ketchup. Well, why not?

Teach your kids about good nutrition. Put the poster of *Canada's Guide to Healthy Eating* (available from your public health unit) on the fridge, and talk with your child about the different food groups. Preschoolers can understand the idea that "your body needs different types of food to grow and be healthy" and enjoy choosing something to eat from each group.

RECOMMENDED READING
What Should I Feed My Kids? The Pediatrician's Guide to Safe and Healthy Food and Growth, by Ronald E. Kleinman, MD, and Michael S. Jellinek, MD, Ballantine Books, 1994. A refreshingly sensible and balanced look at "good eating" for kids.

Perhaps the strongest argument for staying relaxed about picky eating is that, in most cases, this is a "developmental behaviour" that will improve on its own—*if* we don't make an issue out of it. As paediatricians Ronald Kleinman and Michael Jellinek remind us in their book, *What Should I Feed My Kids*, "bizarre as they may seem to you, monotonous or unappealing food preferences are perfectly normal [in children], and in time (perhaps as early as the next meal), will change."

"It is irritating," admits William Gunter. "But my oldest child is 12 now, and I'm seeing the end of the story. He and his friends are starting to grow fast, and they're hungry—they can't be bothered to be picky any more!"

SNACKTIME: WHY CHILDREN NEED MORE THAN "THREE SQUARE MEALS"

'LL NEVER FORGET MY FIRST LIVE DEMONSTRATION of the effect a "low fuel supply" can have on a child's behaviour. My three-year-old had just dissolved into wails over some minor frustration. Nothing unusual there—except that 20 minutes later, he was *still* wailing, with no end in sight. Nothing I did, not comforting, not distracting, not leaving him to run out of steam, could stem the tide of tears.

Until I remembered that he hadn't eaten much lunch, it was 4:00 p.m., and we'd missed snacktime. I waved a piece of cheese under his nose. "I'm *not* hungry!" he howled, wolfing down a bowlful of crackers and cheese. And was instantly cheerful.

Rhona Hanning, an associate professor of nutrition at the University of Toronto, has an extensive background in children's nutrition. She confirms that snacks make an important contribution to a young child's diet: "Preschoolers definitely need snacks. They have very high energy needs, and usually small appetites. They are unlikely to be able to eat enough at one meal to sustain them for four to five hours."

Besides, notes Hanning, "behaviourally, I think regular snacks make for a happier child." (Ain't it the truth!)

But whatever happened to the caution that between-meal snacks would "spoil your supper"? That can actually happen, says Hanning, if the snack is too close to mealtime. "Realistically, though, kids may be clamouring for food by the time you all get home from work and daycare, for example, and they need something to tide them over until dinner."

The solution, says Hanning, is to make sure your child's snacks make a positive contribution to her overall diet. "A handful of candies right before dinner is not a great idea," she explains. "But if you give her a part of her meal—maybe a raw carrot, a drink of milk or her salad—or

SNACKTIME

SNACKS SUPREME
When something "special" is in order, here are some fast and easy favourites:

- "Rolled up" sandwiches: spread bread with peanut butter or softened cream cheese and roll up (you can add an asparagus stalk or some other "prize" inside if your child likes it)
- Popsicles made of fruit juice or a yogurt/juice combination
- Ants on a log: spread celery with cream cheese, dot with raisin "ants"
- Mini-pizzas: spread English muffin halves with tomato sauce, top with grated cheese, melt in the oven, and cut in quarters
- "Face" sandwiches: spread bread with peanut butter or cheese spread, decorate with raisins, carrot strips, alfalfa sprouts, coconut ... (again, whatever he will eat)
- Yogurt smoothies: "milkshakes" made from blended yogurt, fruit and milk (add sugar to taste)
- "Okay, this isn't terribly nutritious," confesses Hanning, "but my kids really like 'spiders'—you slice the ends of hotdog wieners lengthwise into thin strips (but leave the middle intact), and then microwave them until they kind of curl up ..."

---

something like a piece of fruit or cheese, it doesn't matter if she eats less at dinner. It's all healthy food."

In fact, Hanning points out, "sometimes kids will even eat foods for snacks that they reject at dinner." So if the cooked broccoli or carrots are usually left abandoned on your child's plate, you might try offering raw veggies and dip to munch on at snacktime instead. "This can also be a good time to try something new," suggests Hanning.

Dentists do point out that frequent snacking exposes the teeth to more food acids. From a tooth's viewpoint, the worst eating pattern is "grazing" all day on a non-stop stream of mini-snacks. "Foods that stick to the teeth, like raisins, are usually better eaten as part of a meal, when the saliva flow is greater," adds Hanning.

A possible safety concern with snacking is that children may not be as closely supervised as they are at family meals. Choking is a real danger when children "eat on the run," so have them sit down with their snack and keep an eye on them while they're eating.

Snacks don't have to be fancy or troublesome. "A quarter of a sandwich left over from lunch is just fine," says Hanning. In any case, many preschoolers prefer the basic, time-honoured standbys like fruit, cheese cubes, peanut butter and crackers, whole-grain muffins, fruit yogurt, or cereal with milk.

Snacks don't *always* have to be nutritionally perfect, either, reassures Hanning. "It's okay to have a food treat now and then; it's just that you want to limit the amount so that, overall, the diet is healthy." Hanning suggests looking for sweets that also offer some food value, "like oatmeal cookies or peanut butter Rice Krispies squares paired with a glass of milk, rather than marshmallow puffs and cola."

And how about us grown-ups? Maybe we can learn something from the way a well-timed snack can smooth out a child's mood. How many of us, for example, get a little crabby while preparing dinner? Yes, it's true that we're tired, that the traffic was bad, that we're in a hurry and the kids are underfoot. But it's also been a long time since lunch, and low blood sugar does nothing for a person's patience. Better go raid the snack tray.

Learning to Behave:
Positive Discipline for Preschoolers

Kate Williams

NOW THAT YOUR CHILD'S MEMORY, verbal understanding and ability to control his behaviour are developing, your discipline skills can be put into action. Most parents have a lot of questions about discipline (and will until their kids leave home!). What are appropriate expectations for a preschooler? What kind of discipline methods are effective? What am I really trying to teach him, anyway?

If you haven't thought much yet about your discipline goals and methods, now is a good time to start clarifying your ideas. When parents do this, they often realize that while in the *short* term they'd just like their children to do what they're told, in the *long* term they want to raise children who can think independently and control their own behaviour. Sometimes, then, our kids need firm direction from us; at other times they need an opportunity to learn *self*-discipline by experiencing the consequences of their own choices. How you respond to your child's behaviour will vary according to the situation, the age and temperament of the child, and even your own needs at the time.

There are many positive ways of guiding children's behaviour, but perhaps the most important method of all is to be aware of our own example! Remember that your relationship with your child—including how you handle conflict and discipline—is his first, most powerful demonstration of how people live and get along together. If you behave the way you would like your child to behave—even when you're angry with him—you are giving him a strong, consistent model to follow as he grows.

"TRUCE!": DEFUSING CONFLICT

N O PARENT COULD WATCH THE "ice cream scene" in the movie *Kramer vs. Kramer* without rueful recognition. In this scene, the son wants ice cream; the father forbids it. As the little boy rebels, the father draws one line after another: don't get down from your chair...don't open that freezer...don't dare touch that ice cream box—only to see each one crossed. No one is surprised when things finally blow up, ending with the boy in his room weeping, the father yelling, the evening ruined.

Power struggles with preschoolers are depressingly common, and whether we (the parents) "win" or "lose," we don't feel good about them. Is there a better way to manage parent–child conflict?

Kathy Lynn, a Vancouver-based parent educator, explains that defiance and balkiness are normal expressions of children's urge to become more independent. "It's important not to take it personally. These kids aren't out to get us, they're out to separate from us and get on with their life."

Lynn observes that power struggles in this age group are "mostly caused by frustration—on both sides. Big people and little people have different goals; your goal may be to catch the bus, while your daughter's goal is to finish her block tower. She can't understand or care about the bus; developmentally it isn't—and shouldn't be—important to her."

From this perspective, we can see that the first step in decreasing conflict is to minimize frustration. Lynn suggests, "Look at your environment. Does it fit your child's needs? A child-friendly environment is important. Time is another frustrator—young kids just fall apart when they're being rushed."

Now about drawing those lines. Parents have to set limits and teach appropriate behaviour—that's our job. But a little diplomacy brought to the task won't weaken the message, and may make it easier for kids to co-operate. Some suggestions from Lynn:

THE STRONG-WILLED CHILD

Four-year-old Mandy and her dad are walking along a city sidewalk. Suddenly, Mandy darts ahead into the crowd. Her father acts decisively: "Mandy, you must stay beside me. If you run ahead again, you will have to hold my hand."

And now, the million-dollar question: Will Mandy do it again?

If your child, like Mandy, is "strong-willed," it's an easy bet. Of *course* she'll do it again! Not only that, but when her father takes her hand, she will struggle, cry, and drag her legs all the way down the block. Tomorrow, too. And the next day.

Research confirms that many temperamental traits are largely inborn. "Negative persistence" (or, more popularly, "stubbornness") is one such trait, and it's a force to be reckoned with. Margaret DeCorte, an Ottawa psychologist, observes, "These kids create such frustration that parents tend to yell and punish more. But because strong-willed children are so focused on their own goals, they respond very poorly to prohibitions and flat commands. And they don't think about consequences, so punishments just don't work very well."

Instead, DeCorte suggests that techniques for defusing conflict are especially important for these children. She also recommends judicious use of reward programs, which give a child a positive reason to want to change his behaviour.

DeCorte also stresses the importance of choosing your battles. "Try to ignore or negotiate minor things. It's very hard on the whole family if you're fighting all day long," says DeCorte.

At the same time, parents of strong-willed kids must be prepared to enforce *essential* limits, no matter how much time and energy it takes. Your willingness to accommodate your child's basic temperament, *and* teach him to respect fundamental ground rules, will help that "stubbornness" mature into determination, persistence and personal integrity.

Try to say "yes" as much as possible. Little kids hear "no" all day long. It's a word that triggers anger, resentment, frustration. But often your blunt "no" can be rephrased to a conditional "yes." Try saying

"After your bath you can watch TV" instead of "No TV. It's bathtime" or "We can go to the park as soon as you clean up these blocks." Says Lynn, "This teaches the kids that some things need to be done first." It also rewards them for doing tasks promptly.

By the same token, many of our critical prohibitions can be expressed as positive directions: "Stop running around!" can become "You must walk carefully on the pool deck." It's not only more pleasant; it also has the advantage of teaching the child what you *want* as well as what you don't want.

Give fair warning before transitions. Many young children have trouble with sudden changes in activity. And when you think about it, would you ask a grown-up to drop a phone call in mid-sentence to come to the dinner table? "Warnings work best with older preschoolers, who are beginning to understand time," says Lynn. Say "Finish up your picture, because we're eating in five minutes." Set a timer if it helps. Young preschoolers may have no idea how long five minutes is, so it may be more helpful to give other cues: "When I'm finished washing the dishes, it will be time to go to Grandma's." And, adds Lynn, "if you say it's time to go now and bundle him all up, don't *you* then stand around talking. Follow your own rules."

Give appropriate choices. Accommodate your child's need to assert herself by allowing her to choose between acceptable alternatives. Some kinds of misbehaviour, too, lend themselves to choices: "We're trying to talk in here. Either play quietly, or go to the playroom if you want to be noisy." (See "Giving Choices," the next chapter, for more detail.)

Lighten up. There's nothing wrong with making good behaviour fun. By all means distract your child with funny songs as you wrestle on the snowsuit. Entice her interest with the unexpected: one father re-called his squirmy preschooler's attention to lunch by knocking on her sandwich:

DISCIPLINE BOOKS: OUR FAVOURITES

The Discipline Book: Everything You Need to Know to Have a Better-Behaved Child—From Birth to Age Ten, by William Sears, MD, and Martha Sears, RN, Little, Brown, 1995

Discipline: Steps to Success, audio book by Kathy Lynn, 1997 (contact Parenting Today, 604-258-9074)

How to Talk So Kids Will Listen and Listen So Kids Will Talk, by Adele Faber and Elaine Mazlish, Avon Books, 1980

Raising Your Child Not by Force But by Love, by Sidney Craig, Westminster Press, 1982.

Without Spanking or Spoiling: A Practical Approach to Toddler and Preschool Guidance, by Elizabeth Crary, Parenting Press, 1993

"Knock, knock! What's in here?" It made for a pleasant meal, eaten with relish.

Have fewer rules. Sometimes we automatically enforce a rule that, on closer examination, isn't essential. Perhaps you struggle to make your three-year-old wear mitts. If he's just playing in the yard, consider whether wearing mitts—or not—could be his responsibility. He'll certainly come in when his hands are cold. "I suggest that parents step back," says Lynn, "and say 'Why do I want him to do this? What would happen if I let him get his own way?'"

On the other hand, we can also get embroiled in pointless discussions about basic rules. Taking prescription medicine is not negotiable. Staying off the road is not negotiable. You can explain why—briefly— but debating the issue with a preschooler is unlikely to be productive.

Bite the bullet. Finally, says Lynn, remember that sometimes it's kinder for everyone to just do what needs to be done and get it over with. "I remember a four-year-old who was exhausted and hyped-up after a birthday party, and had hysterics when it was time to go home. What she needed was for her mother to take charge and get her out of there so she could calm down. Instead, the mother was trying to reflect back her feelings: 'You're really upset about going, aren't you? I wish I could let you stay longer,' and so on. It just prolonged the girl's distress."

As parents, we inevitably make decisions that our children find unpleasant. We can't sugar-coat them all, nor can we avoid all the noisy protests and rebellions that result. That's okay. When kids feel loved, respected, capable and secure, they can take a few lumps. And so can we.

GIVING CHOICES: OPTIONS ENCOURAGE CO-OPERATION

IT'S BEDTIME NOW. Would you like to wear your red pyjamas or your blue pyjamas?" "Do you want your carrots cooked or raw?" "Would you like to take your Raggedy Ann doll or your teddy bear with you when we go to visit Grandma?"

While some preschoolers are more compliant than others, many strongly resist any direct orders. But as many parents have discovered, kids often find it easier to accept our requirements when they have some input into *how* those requirements are carried out. Just like adults, children like to feel they have some options in their daily lives.

"When Ali gets balky about something, often a simple choice is all it takes to turn her mood around," observes her father, Miles Burton. "The other day it was 'No bath!' But when I said, 'You can have food colouring or bubbles,' she got interested. We settled on both!"

Wendy Jeckell, a former early childhood education teacher who is now at home full time with her three children, finds that giving choices can also be a good way to avoid saying no.

"I noticed that sometimes when my children would ask for something, I'd react quickly and say no. They'd want to go over to the park and play, and I'd say no because I was busy getting supper ready. Then they'd whine and dinner would be unpleasant. But I've learned to give myself time to think about it, and then I can give them choices: 'You can play outside in the back yard while I finish supper, or we can go to the park together after supper. You choose.'"

It's important when you offer a choice that you are prepared to live with your child's decision. Don't say "You can have whatever you like for lunch" if you'll be upset when he chooses chocolate cake. In any case, too many choices can be overwhelming for a preschooler. It's usually best to offer two or three possibilities—a cheese sandwich or a

TOO MANY CHOICES!

"Joel, would you like a red apple or a green apple?"

"I don't want an apple."

"Would you like it peeled or with the skin on?"

"I don't want an apple."

"Sliced in pieces or whole?"

"*No apple!*"

It's not magic, and it doesn't always work. Sometimes you have to accept defeat! Does Joel *have* to eat an apple now, for some reason? Then be upfront about it: "Joel, I want you to have some apple before we go to the play because you haven't had any fruit all day and we can't take snacks in with us. Would you like red or green?" Otherwise, it's better to take no for an answer than get drawn into a coercive exchange like this.

Are there other situations where it's best not to persist with choices? Sometimes when preschoolers are upset and out of control, they need us to take charge. They're already overloaded, and decisions, instead of helping them regain control, just add more pressure. Unfortunately, there's no easy way to tell when this is the case. The overtired child, hysterically resisting bedtime, might respond well to a choice: "Do you want to listen to a tape or have a story?" But if not, there's probably not much sense in prolonging the process with more choices. He might just need you to carry him up to bed.

peanut butter sandwich—not the entire contents of the fridge.

What if your child listens to the choices you're offering and refuses all of them? "No red 'jamas, no blue 'jamas! I'm not going to bed!" (This kind of response is, of course, more likely if he's really overtired and desperately needs some sleep!)

"Sometimes I will just reinforce the choices by saying 'Sorry, that wasn't one of your options. Now, do you want the red pyjamas or the blue ones?'" Wendy says. "My children are so used to making these kind of choices that they usually pick one." Or you can move on and offer a different choice: "Okay, I'll pick your pyjamas for you. And while we're putting them on, you can think about which story you'd like."

Even when the issue is non-negotiable—like wearing a seat belt—Wendy notes that there are often ways to build in a small choice. "For example, I might say he could choose which seat he wanted, but that he *had* to buckle up," she explains.

Even children with easygoing personalities who rarely challenge our rules will benefit from the experience of learning to make decisions and discovering how their choices turn out. Although the small choices we give our preschoolers (what shirt to wear, what cereal to buy, what book to borrow from the library) don't seem to bear much relation to the more critical decisions that await them in their teens, Wendy points out that this early practice is important preparation. By offering gradually more complex choices as they grow, we can help our children to develop an essential skill.

Some kinds of choices you can offer your preschooler:

This one or that one: the pink shirt or the yellow shirt, the mushroom soup or the tomato soup, *Babe* or *101 Dalmations*.

Now or another (specified) time: picking up toys, going for a walk, getting hair washed.

Alone or with me: tidying up his toys, lying down for a nap.

Making choices is a maturing process for children. It encourages them to think about the options they have been presented with, and to look ahead as they try to make the best decision. It can also be a positive way for parents to deal with the many small conflicts and issues that come up every day.

"Giving choices as much as possible works really well for our family," says Wendy. "I think it helps us avoid power struggles and challenges that we might otherwise end up in."

ALTERNATIVES TO SPANKING:
HOW TO SET FIRM LIMITS WITHOUT HITTING

HREE-YEAR-OLD JUSTIN, my next-door neighbour, was absorbed in the lovely screeching sound his stick made when scraped against the side of the car. "Justin, stop that!" his father said sharply. He was met with a blank stare, followed by an emphatic *screeeech*! Justin was spanked on the spot.

"I *had* to spank him," his dad said later, genuinely rueful. "He has to learn to mind."

Many of us would prefer not to spank our children. We believe that hurting children—physically or emotionally—is wrong. But when "gentle correction" is ignored and our anger is sparked, spanking may seem the only alternative.

Teri Degler and Dr. Yvonne Kason, collaborators on the book *Love, Limits, and Consequences*, suggest that in fact there are many, many alternatives to spanking. The problem is that, in the heat of the moment, we don't think of them.

WHAT IF I GOOF?

Yes, it's important to be consistent and to follow through when you set a limit. But the "consistency rule" doesn't mean we can't adjust the consequence and apologize when we realize we've overreacted, says Dr. Yvonne Kason. So take a deep breath, reconsider and then say, "Justin, I know I said you must stay on the porch for the rest of the day, but that's not reasonable. I just said that because I was really angry. I want you to stay here until I'm finished washing the car, and then we'll go in for lunch."

"Parents don't have to be perfect," reminds Kason. "It's good for your child to see that when you make a mistake you do what you can to set it right." After all, that's exactly what we're trying to teach *them* to do!

"The key thing is to have a stockpile of consequences ready," says Degler, who knows from her many years' experience as a special education teacher with emotionally disturbed children how challenging children's behaviour can be. "When you're really frustrated and upset, you can't think clearly, but if you have a stockpile in your mind of appropriate consequences you can reach in and grab an alternative before you lose your cool."

What are some of those alternatives?

First, says Dr. Kason, a family physician and psychotherapist, make sure your child understands what's expected of him: "Discipline should include teaching. If a young child pulls a cat's tail, you show him how to pat gently, and explain how rough play hurts the cat."

If the child does understand the limits, but deliberately defies them, then it's time to introduce consequences, say Degler and Dr. Kason:

If the child is misusing a *thing*—using a toy truck to squash his brother's sand castles—then we can take away that object for a specified period of time. (In Justin's case, we take away the stick.)

If the child is misusing a *situation* or *person*—playing roughly, yelling when people are trying to talk—then she can be removed from the situation in a brief "time out" on a special chair, in her room, or right beside you. For children under five, one minute per year of age is enough time, caution Degler and Kason. Often the child can decide how long the time out needs to be: "You can come back when you're ready to play gently." ("Time Out and Time In," the next chapter, discusses this further.)

Sometimes a stronger consequence is needed. Perhaps Justin finds a new stick and deliberately scratches the car *again*. Now, suggests Dr. Kason, you may have to withdraw a privilege: "You didn't listen, so now we won't be going to the park." Degler cautions that this type of

CONSEQUENCES AND PUNISHMENT: WHAT'S THE DIFFERENCE?
Sometimes, it's true, the "consequences" we impose for misbehaviour are simply old-fashioned punishments with a nicer name. But what parent educators call "logical consequences" are quite different. A logical consequence, when you can find one, is a better way to teach appropriate behaviour, because it springs directly from the misbehaviour itself. Some examples:

- Mary colours on her mother's computer screen. *Punishment:* Mary is not allowed to watch TV for the rest of the day. *Consequence:* Mary's crayons are put away. For the next week, she can colour only under supervision, "so we know you're using them properly."
- Christopher rides his tricycle into the road. *Punishment:* No stories at bedtime. *Consequence:* Christopher has to stay in the back yard (when he plays outside) until the next day. Before going out front again, he shows his mother where he is allowed to walk or ride.
- Kylie spits her chocolate milk across the table. *Punishment:* Sent to her room. *Consequence:* Dad takes away the milk, "since you're not interested in drinking it," and gives her the dishcloth to wipe up the dribbles.

A good logical consequence:

- is closely related to what the child has done
- helps the child learn about responsibility
- fits the child's stage of development
- for young children especially, happens right away, not hours or days later
- gives the child a chance to try again after the consequence
- is not humiliating or painful

It can be hard to think of a logical consequence, especially on the spot. If you feel that some kind of consequence is required (and remember, often a simple correction or reminder is enough), it's okay to take a few minutes to consider your options.

consequence needs to be fairly immediate: "If he does something wrong in the morning and the consequence is no TV that afternoon, the child doesn't see the connection between the misdeed and the punishment." The best consequences follow logically from the "mistake": "Now we have to pick up all these cards, and there won't be any time left to play another game before dinner."

Degler and Dr. Kason also stress the importance of troubleshooting— a preventive approach to behaviour problems. Preschoolers often misbehave when they are tired, hungry or desperate for attention; so regular naps, snacks and time with you will help keep them on an even keel. Changes in routines and exciting events may also challenge their self-control. If Emily is cranky and hyper after a long day at the zoo, a soothing bath and bed will do her more good than "discipline."

It's important to fit your approach to the child. Some children almost never require more than a stern word, while others will struggle against the rules constantly. Degler and Dr. Kason suggest that, for these more challenging children, it's especially important to set up a clear structure, so everyone knows just what the limits are, and to follow through with consequences. Says Dr. Kason, "More difficult kids need more consistent discipline. When they test the limits, there has to be a follow-through with a consequence so they know those limits are real."

Degler adds, "Consistency doesn't mean that there can't be exceptions. Kids can understand that you may relax the rules on holidays or for another special occasion. But when you *do* set the limit, you have to follow through."

Dr. Kason concludes, "The very most important thing is unconditional love. Children need to feel that they are loved, even when they do something bad. There's a lot of room for error in parenting, but this is essential."

TIME OUT AND TIME IN: WHEN YOU NEED A BREAK IN THE ACTION

RIENDS ARE VISITING, and four-year-old Melissa is getting pretty wound up. Despite her mother's cautions, Melissa's disruptive behaviour—yelling, running through the crowded room, throwing toys—is escalating. Mom takes Melissa by the hand and leads her out of the room, saying "Melissa, I asked you to play quietly. We can't talk when you yell, and you could trip or hurt somebody when you run in here. You'll have to go to time out and calm down."

Melissa is installed in a chair in the (unoccupied) living room, without toys or company. The timer is set for four minutes (one minute for each year of age). Although Melissa grumbles and fusses at first, she stays in her chair. When the timer rings, her mother arrives. "Okay, Melissa, you can come back and play now. I know that this time you'll be more careful and quiet."

This is "time out," a very popular discipline technique, which, says Carolyn Webster-Stratton in her book *The Incredible Years* (Umbrella Press, 1992), "is actually an extreme form of parental ignoring in which children are removed for a brief period from all sources of...reinforcement, especially adult attention." Rather than a punishment, time out is most often promoted as a "cooling-off" period for children, which interrupts their negative behaviour and whatever stimulation is encouraging it. Done correctly, its proponents say, it helps children learn to control their behaviour without damaging their self-esteem. But there are pitfalls to time out that parents should recognize.

"It takes a lot of persistence at first," advises Judy McCann-Beranger, a parent educator whose company, People Concepts, is based in Charlottetown, P.E.I. "Until children understand that you really mean it, they may resist going to time out, leave time out repeatedly, or have tantrums during time out." Parents introducing time out as a

GO TO YOUR ROOM

Should you send a child to his or her room for time out? Opinion is mixed. Some sources warn that a child might "enjoy" a time out in her room: she has too much freedom there, and access to interesting toys. Time out, they argue, should be boring, not fun. But if the intent of time out is to interrupt the misbehaviour, not to punish the child, does it matter if she has a nice time? One mother recalls, "I sent Robby for a time out in his room and when the timer went off, I called to him that he could come out. But he didn't. I thought he must be sulking in there, but when I peeked in, he was on his bed with a stack of books, having a lovely quiet time to himself. And that was what he needed. When he reappeared fifteen minutes later, he was his old happy self again."

Other parents find time out works better when they keep their child close by. Some preschoolers find it frightening to be sent that far away (especially if the bedroom is on another floor of the house), and some need a parent's watchful eye until they regain control.

consequence for misbehaviour need to plan how they will enforce it without giving the child a lot of extra attention.

McCann-Beranger also stresses that it's important to ensure that positive interaction with a child outweighs negative consequences like time out: "Don't just focus on the negative behaviour. Model the behaviours you'd like to see, and make sure the child experiences positive consequences to her good behaviour."

Webster-Stratton lists a few common misuses of time out:

Time out is too long. Webster-Stratton stresses, "Time outs longer than five minutes are not more effective." Often children can even decide for themselves how long is enough: "Come on back when you're ready to be gentle with the dog."

Time out is used too often. It's best, says Webster-Stratton, to use time out for just a few "high-intensity" misbehaviours.

The child is not given a chance to try again, or is allowed to use time out to avoid doing a task. After time out, the child should be invited "back to the fold."

McCann-Beranger suggests that parents interested in trying time out give it a trial for a few weeks, and then assess its effectiveness. "Every child is different, and time out doesn't work equally well with all children."

While time out is certainly preferable to spanking or other painful, humiliating or frightening punishments, not all child development experts are enthusiastic about its use.

Otto Weininger, a prominent child psychologist at the Ontario Institute for Studies in Education (Toronto), says, "I don't think there is a place for time out in this age group. Even though it's not intended, I think children see time out as parental rejection, as a message that they're not good enough or their feelings are not acceptable."

Weininger explains that preschoolers rely on their parents to help them deal with their upsetting feelings: "There are so many things children are trying to do and learn at this age, and much of their anger is frustration at their lack of success. When a child is having trouble, can't control himself or does something aggressive, then removing him from the parent withdraws

TIME OUT FOR PARENTS
Sometimes it's the grown-ups who need time out! Saying "I'm so angry right now I can't think straight! I'm going to my room to calm down, and then we'll figure out what to do about the paints on the couch" sends a strong model of self-control and problem-solving to your little darling, and may save you from actions you'd regret. Those few minutes, used to "look before you leap," will help you use your parenting skills effectively. Just make sure that you are leaving your child in a safe environment—she may need to be in her room while you're in yours.

the 'containment' the parent would normally provide, at a time when he needs it the most."

As an alternative, Weininger suggests a "time in" with the parent: the child is kept close to the parent (or caregiver) until she has regained control. There are a number of ways this can be done, notes Weininger. "You can say 'I'm sorry that you're feeling bad, but you hurt Jason. I want you to come sit right beside me till you're feeling better.' You can then sit the child on a chair close beside you while you continue washing the dishes. You are keeping everyone 'safe' while helping her to settle down. Or if the situation itself—an overstimulating play setting or too many people visiting—is overwhelming the child, you can have a time out *together*—go upstairs and read a story while the child calms down."

"I go sit on the stairs *with* my three-year-old," says Janine McCue. "It keeps him from leaving, but it also gives us a quiet, private moment out of the fray. At first, he's mad, but soon he's ready to be cuddled. And then we talk about what needs to happen when he goes back."

Alone or with you, providing a few moments "out of the fray" is what time out does best.

"I DON'T HAFTA!": PRESCHOOL BACKTALK

HE FIRST TIME A TWO-YEAR-OLD bursts out with, "*Give* me a *break!*," it's really kind of cute...but the appeal quickly fades with constant repetition. Many of us have rejected child-rearing philosophies that insist children should be "seen and not heard." We explain things to our kids, encourage them to express their feelings and think for themselves. But authoritarian parenting may suddenly look pretty good when a perfectly reasonable request is met with a pint-sized sneer: "I don't hafta, you dirty pee!" After all, *we* wouldn't have dared talk to our parents that way.

Martin and Georgine Nash run the Sheppard Adlerian Counselling and Education Centre in Toronto, where they offer parenting courses, counselling and psychotherapy. They agree that parent–child relationships have changed—but they think it's for the better. Says Georgine, "Children today will not accept the sort of forced respect of parents that was the norm twenty or thirty years ago. Children know that they deserve respect and understand that they have rights. Therefore when they feel that they have been treated disrespectfully, they feel they have the right to retaliate."

Adds Martin, "Even if you are successful at being authoritarian, your child will learn to deal with authority by being submissive. In the long run, is that what we want?"

Okay, so we won't return to Victorian times. Yet we do want to teach our children that insults and name-calling are not a good way to relate to people. What can we do?

First of all, as child psychologist Penelope Leach points out in her classic guide, *Your Baby and Child*, if a child who is truly angry and upset screams out an insult, she is, in fact, using considerable self-control and doing what we have been trying to teach her, "... to use words

SWEARING

"We were at a restaurant out in the country with my son and his family," recalls grandfather Bill Hoffman, "and his three-year-old daughter was looking dreamily out the window. Then suddenly I hear this matter-of-fact little voice chirping, 'There's those f***ing cows again.'"

Luckily, this grandpa found the whole scene pretty amusing. But plenty of adults look askance when swearing comes out of the mouths of babes. And kids, even if their first experiments with swear words are completely innocent, quickly pick up on the interesting reaction these new words can provoke. So once it starts, it can quickly accelerate. Some tips for gently discouraging bad language:

- **Watch your own mouth.** It's obvious, but still important. Many of us have no idea how often we actually do swear, until we hear our children's perfect imitations.
- **Don't overreact.** A simple "That's not a very nice word and I don't want you to say it," followed by determined ignoring of the inevitable "testing" repetitions that follow (or maybe leaving the room if it continues), is probably more effective than getting all hot and bothered. It's hard to play to an indifferent audience.
- **Explain a bit about "situational appropriateness,"** especially if swearing is not that big a deal to you. "I know they are just words, but many people are very upset by swear words. And I don't want to make other people feel bad, so I don't swear when I'm around people who might mind."
- **Do distinguish between provocative swearing and truly upset feelings.** "My four-year-old arrived home from kindergarten one day with a face like a stormcloud," recalls one mother. "He was practically shaking with pent-up rage. Finally he wailed, 'Dammit! Shit!' and burst into tears, and sobbed out an account of some injustice at school. I didn't even mention the swearing. I just cuddled him up and let him cry."

instead of blows. The trouble is that having taught these lessons parents often don't much like the angry *words* either." When we remember how hard it is for adults to express rage in a non-hurtful way, we'll realize it's not fair to expect much sophistication from a four-year-old.

The child who is "sassy" is another kettle of fish. He is discovering that certain words can make him feel powerful—and that they can have a pretty interesting effect on his parents. For this kind of "backtalk," the following suggestions may be helpful:

Model the behaviour you would like to see, say the Nashes. Talk respectfully to your children and mate, even when you are angry. Learn to use I-messages that say how *you* feel, rather than resorting to name-calling and accusations. If you call him a "noisy little pest," don't be surprised when he returns the favour.

Model self-respect. You have rights too. Martin Nash suggests, "If a child talks to you disrespectfully, say: 'I am not willing to stay here and be called names,' and then remove yourself from the scene." (Go read in the bathroom.)

Avoid power struggles. The parental strong-arm, say the Nashes, is best reserved for matters of life and limb. Georgine notes, "Children will often try to engage a parent in an argument. If the parent argues back it reinforces the child's mistaken belief that winning the argument is the important thing." In other words, not only do power struggles leave you both feeling rotten, they have a long shelf-life. You may win this one, but just wait until your strait-laced Aunt Mildred comes to visit...

Don't let backtalk sidetrack you from the original issue. If the messy room is forgotten because of an intervening lecture on talking back, the child will learn that being saucy is a good diversionary tactic.

Allow the older preschooler to negotiate at times, *if* he speaks respectfully. Make it clear to him why you are (or are not) being flexible: ("Okay, we can wait until after this show to go shopping—because you explained to me quietly and politely how much you love it," or "I'm sorry, but that kind of talk will not change my mind.")

Explain that people's feelings can be hurt. It's best to do this later, during a quiet, friendly time. You might say something like: "You know how if someone hits you, that hurts. Well, if someone says mean things to you, that can hurt you on the inside—it makes you feel sad. We don't want to hurt anyone, so we try not to say mean things to people."

Finally, as is true about so many parenting issues, it's important not to take our preschooler's words too personally. One mother was brought to tears at the end of a stressful day when her four-year-old announced scornfully: "I don't have to listen to you. You're just a stupid mommy!" She recalls, "It tapped all my insecurities and my resentment of our society's devaluing of stay-home mothers. But to Jake, stupid was just the only really bad thing he knew to call me... and mommy is simply what I am."

Backtalk is tiresome to deal with. But if we can help our kids gradually learn to express their feelings and viewpoints without the mudslinging, perhaps they will grow into adults who can stand up for themselves *and* respect the rights of others.

TEMPER, TEMPER: DEALING WITH TANTRUMS

W E'RE NEARING THE END OF A LONG DAY at Marineland and we've paused in our trek to watch the bears prowl around their den several feet below us. Before I can stop her, five-year-old Claire takes the last marshmallow out of the bag and tosses it to one of the bears. The bear scoops it up in a massive paw and stands on two legs, examining it closely.

Cameron, age three, suddenly hurls himself onto the grass. He *wanted* that marshmallow. He was going to eat that marshmallow, and he wants me, right now, to climb into the bear's den and retrieve it. And if I won't go in and get it, he'll go in himself.

Cameron's not just saying this, he's screaming it. There are now more people looking at Cameron than at the bears. Finally I pick him up, put him in the stroller and push him away, still screaming. By the time we reach the nearest food stand, his screams have turned into sobs, and when I suggest we all have an ice cream cone, he nods, the tears still running down his face.

It's easy (with 20-20 hindsight) to identify the factors that brought on Cameron's tantrum: a long day with lots of excitement and stimulation that left him tired out; separation from his mother (who was off with an older child on one of the rides in another part of the park); being hungry and watching what he must have thought was the last piece of available food disappearing into the bear's den.

Lorraine Gilman, a parent resource worker with Information Children (at Simon Fraser University in B.C.), says this kind of situation can easily lead to "out-of-control feelings and a tantrum." What's needed: "A cuddle, a snack, a rest, some time away from the excitement and the stressful situation" to help the child regain control. Gilman reminds parents that preschoolers, with their limited social and verbal skills, might not recognize or know how to tell you when things are getting to be too much for them.

Temper tantrums aren't always so predictable; some catch parents completely by surprise. Marcia Cudmore says that, for four-year-old Bethany, "making her own decisions is a big deal right now. If I put out the wrong colour underwear for her, that can trigger a major tantrum. It seems so trivial to me, but it's important to her to make her own decisions about things—including her underwear."

Marcia finds that often the best thing to do is back off and not try to rush or push Bethany when she's in the throes of a tantrum. "There is little point in trying to reason with her—she's too emotional to be able to listen."

At other times she has to remove Bethany from the situation. "Sometimes at bedtime, Bethany's older brother is already brushing his teeth and she decides she wants to brush hers too—right now. So she starts trying to push him away from the sink, and when he refuses to move the tantrum starts." When that happens, Cudmore picks Bethany up and takes her to her room until she can calm down and be a bit more reasonable about the bathroom schedule. "It can take a long time," Cudmore admits. "Part of the problem is that she's tired, too."

These are approaches that Gilman describes as "variations on ignoring." She explains: "Everyone has a slightly different strategy, and a lot depends on the individual parents and child. But many parents find it helps to either walk into another room themselves, or put the child in his bedroom and say, 'Come on out when you've cooled down.'" Younger preschoolers, especially, may calm down more easily when the parent stays close by, but it's still a good idea to move away from the tantrum "trigger"—whether it's the bathroom or a bear's den—to a more neutral or private place. Unlike toddlers, who have often forgotten about the original frustration by the time they've finished crying, preschoolers may want to talk about the situation once the hysteria passes.

An angry preschooler in the midst of a tantrum may strike out at a

TIPS FOR TANTRUM PREVENTION

You can't head off every tantrum at the pass, but advance planning and parental alertness can reduce the number you have to deal with.

- **Take care of the basics.** Once past toddlerhood, parents can get out of the habit of keeping track of when their kids ate last, how far they've walked, or how long they've been cooped up inside. Avoid the hungry–tired–stressed-out syndrome by helping your child regulate the pace of her day.
- **Give warning before transitions.** An abrupt change from one (absorbing) activity to another is a common tantrum trigger. Try to give your child time to finish up and switch gears.
- **Give choices.** Underwear colour won't be an issue between you if she picks her own, and a simple choice (peanut butter or ham?) can head off less reasonable demands (roast chicken).
- **Explain your expectations in advance.** If candy at the checkout has been a source of conflict, some advance coaching may help: "We're buying groceries, and you can choose which cereal and which crackers we buy, but we're not buying candy, and I don't want you to ask me for it."
- **Observe, and avoid, the big triggers.** Do you know it will make him crazy to go to a toy store while you pick out a present for your nephew, without getting anything for himself? If you can, save the shopping for a time when you can go alone. Many of these situations become easier once children get a bit older.

parent or anyone close by. A husky five-year-old who is really mad can cause real pain, and the shock of being physically attacked by your child can be pretty upsetting, too. Don't hit back, but do protect yourself, leaving the room if necessary. Marcia find it helps to keep repeating (as often as necessary), "I know you're upset but you can't hurt people." She says: "You have to remember that they're so upset that they're being irrational. Usually after they calm down they come over and hug you and tell you they're sorry."

Gilman finds that children who are very angry often calm down quite quickly if a parent acknowledges it: "You're really angry, I can see how mad you are." She suggests that, once the child calms down, the parent could suggest better ways to express these strong feelings—such as drawing an angry picture.

Tantrums in public places are probably the worst for parents. "I remember standing at a cash register with a five-year-old lying on the floor beside me, his hands wrapped around my ankles while he cried because I wouldn't buy him the action figure he wanted," recalls Tina Miner. "There is no really good way to handle this situation! And you can't help but feel self-conscious about your audience.

"But I just finished making my purchases, peeled his hands off my legs, pulled him to his feet and walked out to the car with him. I turned on the radio and didn't say a word. By the time we got home, he'd stopped crying."

Gilman says the message in these situations is this: "You can have a tantrum if you want, but I'm simply not going to give in to it. When you're finished, we'll go on with what we're doing." Since it takes a lot of energy to throw a good tantrum, most children who are using this to "get their way" will soon give it up if it doesn't work.

"It's humiliating to have a child having a tantrum in public," Gilman admits, "but it's important to keep your cool—perhaps by counting to ten or asking your partner to take over while you walk away." After all, the last thing an out-of-control child needs is an out-of-control parent!

Staying calm also allows the parent to get a better perspective on the situation, according to Gilman. "Children have tantrums for a lot of different reasons, and what you do about the tantrum depends on what else is going on." As Marcia Cudmore says: "I can't give a consistent answer to how I deal with tantrums, because each situation is different. I think it's important to try to understand what she's feeling and what she's upset about—and then you can figure out how to handle it."

"BREAK IT UP!": SIBLING SQUABBLES

ITH SIX CHILDREN under the age of nine, Colleen Francisci has lots of experience with sibling squabbles. She finds that, as many parents do, her biggest dilemma is when to "let them work it out" and when to intervene. Resolving arguments with siblings and peers is part of the process of learning social skills, but there are times when parents need to intervene to prevent children from being hurt or victimized.

Francisci's five-year-old, Sam, and her three-year-old, Ellen, generally play together quite well, but do fight over toys. Francisci says she tries to ignore the fighting as much as possible to allow them to find their own solutions, but admits that this doesn't always work.

"You have to pay attention to the tone of the fight," she says. "If you're listening, you can tell when one child is getting so upset that he or she is about to lose it. Then I'll step in and try to help them negotiate."

Her favourite approach is the "five-minute rule. Ellen can have the toy for five minutes and then Sam gets it for five minutes. If they won't go for that, I sometimes take the toy away altogether."

Michael Brown says fighting over toys is also the big challenge for his children—Rachel, five, and Shaun, three. "Even though Rachel is older, if she has a toy that Shaun wants, he'll just march right in and grab it from her. She'll try to negotiate and make deals with him, but he tends to just hang on tight to whatever it is."

While Francisci says she is quite comfortable letting her children sort out most of their disagreements, Brown admits that he sometimes has a hard time staying out of the fights. "My first instinct is to jump in and solve it. I have to hold myself back and let them sort it out—I keep reminding myself that if I always jump in at the beginning of an argument, they'll never learn to work things out."

Jill Kreppner, the mother of three-year-old Jaimie and five-year-old

THE MEDIATOR: HOW TO HELP WITHOUT TAKING OVER

It's true that if we're constantly swooping in with our own ready-made solutions to our children's conflicts ("Fine, then neither of you can watch TV," "Okay, Robbie picks today and Lisa picks tomorrow"), we aren't giving our kids a chance to learn how to work things out. But leaving them to struggle on alone hardly seems very educational, either.

There is a way to intervene in a way that coaches kids to negotiate with each other. It's time-consuming, sometimes frustrating, and no busy parent can possibly manage it all the time. But now and then, at a well-chosen moment, try playing mediator:

DAD: Hey, kids, what's the problem?

KIDS (clamouring together): He hit me! I did not! Send him to his room! But she said . . .

DAD: Whoa! One at a time! Jason, you look mad. How come?

JASON: Sarah won't let me watch *Real Monsters*. She just came in and changed the channel!

DAD: Sarah? Jason wanted to watch *Real Monsters*.

SARAH: But I've been planning to watch *Sailor Moon* all day.

DAD (summarizing the problem): So you want to watch one show, Sarah, and Jason wants to watch another.

JASON: And I was here first!

SARAH: So what! I've been waiting all day!

DAD: Is there anything we could do that would be fair for both of you?

JASON/SARAH: (Blank looks)

DAD: Like, could we tape one show or does one of these shows play some other time? Or is there a third show you'd both like to watch?

SARAH: Well, I like *Real Monsters* but I don't want to miss *Sailor Moon*.

DAD: If I taped it, you could watch it after supper . . .

SARAH: Okay. But tape it quick, Daddy, we're going to miss it. . . .

Does it always work out so nicely? In your dreams. But sometimes it does. And it focuses kids on looking for solutions, rather than winning and losing.

Dylan, says she thinks it's important to be aware of your children's different personalities. "Jaimie, for example, is a real peacemaker, and will often give in to Dylan just to keep the peace. Dylan, of course, just says, 'Okay, I win, we'll do it my way.'" Kreppner worries that if all their disagreements follow this pattern, Jaimie may end up giving in this way all her life, so she encourages Jaimie to stand up for herself.

When she does get "assertive" though, it can sometimes be even more of a problem. "Because Jaimie doesn't have the verbal skills Dylan does, she tends to resort to scratching or hitting and of course I can't permit that. I have to remember that she's just learning. We sit down and discuss these things a lot."

Kreppner has also noticed that Jaimie is much better at standing up for herself when dealing with other children in the neighbourhood: "She has this friend, Alyssa, who is a couple of years older than her. I heard Alyssa telling Jaimie that if she didn't do things her way, she was going to break her toy. Jaimie just said, 'Go away. Go home. I'm not playing with you.' She'll give in to Dylan but not Alyssa."

All three parents agree that if a fight escalates to hitting or other physical attacks, it's time to intervene.

"At our house, hitting is an automatic time out," says Kreppner. In other words, she escorts the culprit to her room and says: "You can come back out when you're ready to play without hitting."

BROTHERLY...LOVE?
Parents often find fighting among siblings the most discouraging part of parenting. Yet a certain amount of squabbling—quite a lot of squabbling, actually—is perfectly normal. What do kids fight about? Parents surveyed by Nancy Samalin for her book, *Loving Each One Best*, offered an overwhelming array of mostly (from an adult viewpoint) nonsensical conflicts, including:

- Who sits where
- Who holds the remote control
- Who turns on the light
- Who gets to lie on Mommy's pillow
- Who gets in the car first
- Whose blue coat is bluer...

So now you know. It's not just *your* kids!

FURTHER READING ON
SIBLING SQUABBLES
Stop It, You Two!, an
audiotape by
Canadian parent edu-
cator Kathy Lynn can
be ordered from
Parenting Today (604)
258-9074.

*Loving Each One Best:
A Caring and Practical
Approach to Raising
Siblings*, by Nancy
Samalin (Bantam
Books, 1996). This
book on sibling
rivalry offers support,
strategies, and comic
relief.

*Siblings without
Rivalry*, by Adele
Faber and Elaine
Mazlish, Avon Books,
1987. Still a classic.

Francisci says she offers comfort and understanding to the child who has been hit instead of
getting angry at the child who did the hitting. "It
can be more complicated than who hit who.
Sometimes Sam has been teasing and provoking
Ellen until she gets frustrated and punches him,
and then he runs to tell me. So I give him some
sympathy about his injuries, remind Ellen not to
hit, and they often then go off and play happily."

When arguments erupt into a free-for-all,
many parents find a blanket rule works well: "if
there's physical fighting, *everyone* goes to time
out." This doesn't necessarily have to be puni-
tive—you can just announce you're separating
everyone to keep them safe—but it does keep
you out of the "whose fault" debate.

While Francisci's children—with a houseful of
siblings—quickly learn the skill of fighting and
making up again, it can be harder for only children or preschoolers who haven't yet spent a lot
of time with peers. They might feel devastated
when a friend tries to take away a toy or refuses
to play the game they want, or become overly
bossy in an attempt win every argument. Be pre-
pared to show them a little extra guidance and understanding—they may
need time to become proficient at coping with these everyday problems.

As Kreppner points out: "Younger children don't really play
together—at best they play side by side. But preschoolers really want to
play with each other, to interact, and that inevitably leads to disagreements and fights. As parents, we need to have some patience with the
learning process."

Imagination in Action:
Learning through Play

SEAN IS MAKING AN ELABORATE "thing" out of Lego. Laura and Candace are decked out in their mother's old dresses and jewellery, giggling and talking in high-pitched princess voices. Amy is filling up a hole in the back yard with water, then throwing pine cones in to "swim." Justin is just lying in a sunny patch on the floor, humming quietly and twirling his stuffed dog in his hands. Such different activities, yet we call them all "play." And they are all important to a child's well-being, learning and development.

What do children gain from play? It can be easier for adults to see the learning kids get from more structured play: using construction toys, drawing, doing puzzles. Play activities that include counting, sorting, spatial reasoning, shape identification and other "pre-reading" and "pre-math" skills clearly help children learn concepts that will have direct application when they start school.

But children also need opportunities for pretend play, exuberant running and climbing, and private daydreaming. They need to play alone, with their parents and (increasingly as they get older) with other children. Through pretend play they try out adult roles, come to terms with fears, explore developmental issues like power and belonging. Physical play encourages both large and fine-motor development, builds confidence and stamina, releases pent-up energy and frustration. Play with other children is an exciting, demanding "learning lab" for social skills.

Without a single "educational" toy, children at play learn so much: science, assertiveness, co-operation, creative thought, problem-solving, emotional equilibrium. Do join in with your preschooler's play now and then. It's a delightful window into his world.

"LET'S PRETEND": ROLE-PLAYING AND FANTASIES

ARILYN CALLS FOUR-YEAR-OLD Christopher to come downstairs: it's time for their trip to the bank. He arrives wearing a pair of underpants on top of his track pants and a long blue towel draped around his neck.

"Oh, Christopher, you can't come to the bank dressed like that," she protests.

Her son glares at her. "I'm not Christopher, I'm Superman."

So Superman goes to the bank with his mother, chattering all the way about the children he saved from an earthquake the day before and the places he'll fly to after they are finished at the bank.

Marilyn smiles when she tells the story. "He's certainly got an active imagination," she says.

That description fits most preschoolers. This is the age when pretending, role-playing and other forms of imaginative play take precedence over most other activities. As Toronto child psychotherapist Jacqui Gajewski explains, "Play is the natural medium of expression for children this age. They can't talk things out the way an adult might, so instead they play it out."

She describes a number of different things that kids learn through pretending. "Preschoolers watch what other people are doing and imitate them in an attempt to assimilate what they are seeing—they play at being other people. This is how they learn about social roles and begin to understand the perspective of other people."

A child might come home from a visit to the doctor and proceed to immunize all his dolls and stuffed animals. After she's attended a wedding, another might spend the day organizing friends and toys into a wedding party, while she takes on the role of the minister.

"Children often switch roles back and forth," adds Gajewski. "If two

IMAGINARY FRIENDS

Jonathan Kilmartin, now 11, has vivid memories of his imaginary friend, Keek. "I met Keek when I was four. I was given a set of boats and trailers as a present, and Keek was the owner of the marina. I played with him every day. Keek repaired the boats, sold me parts, and sometimes went to the rescue if a person ran out of gas or something."

How real was Keek? Did he seem like a real person? "Sort of," says Jonathan. "It wasn't like he was sitting there beside me, but he seemed real enough to have conversations with and to play with."

Jonathan played with Keek the most at a time when he had no close friends in the neighbourhood. As Jonathan grew older, and especially when his best friend, Danny, moved into the neighbourhood, play with Keek grew less frequent. "I guess Keek's retired now," adds Jonathan.

In the American Academy of Pediatrics book *Caring for Your Baby and Young Child*, Steven P. Shelov reassures parents about the imaginary friends preschoolers sometimes conjure up with startling vividness: "Don't be concerned...that these phantom friends may signal loneliness or emotional upset; they're actually a very creative way for your child to sample different activities, lines of conversation, behaviour and emotions."

If your preschooler has a special but imaginary friend, enjoy the experience as a wonderful demonstration of his imagination and a way for him to enrich his pretend play.

children are playing mother and baby, the one who is being the mother may switch over to being the baby after a little while. They're just trying things out."

She explains that these experiments with other roles are an important part of the children's growing sense of self. They're trying to understand who they are, how they differ from other people, and what they might potentially become. Imaginative play helps them find answers to these questions.

As well, pretend play can help a child work through inner conflicts and stressful situations. "A typical example," says Gajewski, "is the three-year-old who has a new baby in the family. She might play with a baby doll and pretend that a bad man comes and takes the baby away. Then Superman or a good fairy arrives and rescues the baby."

This kind of play expresses the child's ambivalent feelings about the baby—anger and resentment that the baby is taking up so much of her parents' time and attention, mixed with love and affection for this tiny new person. Those feelings are never fully resolved, so the scenario may be played out over and over again in different ways.

Because imaginative play is so important to preschoolers, it's worth the effort for parents to create an environment that encourages it. Doing this means giving kids freedom. Gajewski urges parents not to censor their children's play. "Parents may feel very uncomfortable if they see their child playing very aggressively, perhaps hitting a doll or having all kinds of tragedies happen to the teddy bear. They'll say 'Oh, come on, play nice.' But that causes the child's anger to go underground—he needs to be allowed to play out both good and bad feelings."

Superhero play—very popular with young boys—does need some parental supervision to make sure kids don't get carried away and hurt each other. But it's not hard to understand why a four-year-old would get a lot of satisfaction out of pretending to be as strong and powerful as a superhero! You may need to set firm limits on the behaviour ("No actual hitting or throwing. This is just pretend.") and even redirect the action ("How about if you're both on the same team?") to keep things safe, but, again, try not to censor their imagination.

To encourage play, parents can take part in their child's pretending games. Their participation, though, should be at the child's invitation and should follow his lead. "Remember, it's his game, not yours. Let him take you into the scenarios he needs to play out," suggests Gajewski.

Reading aloud to children, especially fairy tales and fantasy stories, helps to develop this playful imagination. And keeping plenty of props around, such as old clothes (shirts, hats, purses, aprons, etc.) and play furniture and equipment (cradles, pots and pans, doctor's kits, etc.) may provide the spark that sets off "Let's pretend." Children also enjoy using dolls, small play figures and puppets in their play, but imaginative kids will play with almost anything. I've watched my children have long conversations with a family of bath sponges, and listened while the mommy potato explained to the baby potato that they can't go outside because it's raining. And any parent who's tried to avoid toy weapons can ruefully describe how ingeniously kids can fashion a gun or light-sabre from anything from toast to Lego!

"Parents sometimes don't realize how important pretend play is for children," Gajewski concludes. It may seem less "productive" than activities that focus on learning numbers, shapes or letters, but in fact children learn a great deal from imaginative play. And the best contribution parents can make is to create an accepting atmosphere where their preschoolers can give their imaginations free rein—even sometimes making a trip to the bank with Superman.

RUN, JUMP, CLIMB: BODY POWER!

PRESCHOOLER DOESN'T QUIETLY OBSERVE her world—she jumps on it, rides her bike through it and slides under it. She gets into it. Her parents get into it too. Take Alison Forestell. As she chopped her daughter Geneva's bicycle out of the ice in the bottom of the garden shed one frigid morning, she thought to herself, "This is crazy. I must be crazy."

Not crazy. Just eager to give Geneva the chance to get outside and be active when she feels that need to go.

Parents are constantly looking for ways to add active play to their children's routines, and it's not only to wear them out so that they'll be tired at bedtime (although there's that, too!). Watching a preschooler scramble up a climber, a parent might think that the benefits of active play are mostly physical. After all, young children are developing co-ordination, balance and motor skills. But that's just the beginning. As Terry Orlick, Ottawa sports psychologist and author of *Nice on My Feelings* (Creative Bound Press, 1995), says, "At this age, children learn so much through their active play—all kinds of things about perception, movement and interaction."

Pam Ellis is often witness to this "physical education." Her five-year-old daughter, Erin, spends a lot of time on the go—exploring, playing hide-and-seek, skipping. "She doesn't walk, she skips everywhere she goes." On summer expeditions around their home, Erin runs around and finds lots of interesting bugs and flowers. In the fall, she rakes leaves and builds forts with her older sister. In winter the forts are made of snow, and the front lawn is converted to a mini-skating rink. Even rainy days are busy with puddle-jumping and worm-hunting. Says Pam, "Through all this active play, all sorts of 'how and why' questions come up. We can see her imagination and her observation skills growing along with her co-ordination and strength. She is very aware of the world around her."

PLAYGROUND SAFETY
What could be better than a playground full of climbers, swings and slides? A playground designed with safety as well as fun in mind. The Canadian Standards Association introduced Canada's first playground safety guidelines in 1990, but many play structures still have a long way to go.

Some highlights of the standards, to help you assess your local (or backyard) playground:

- **Most injuries result from falls. Check for guardrails around high platforms and slip-resistant surfaces on ladders. Equipment should be surrounded with a shock-absorbing surface like pea gravel—concrete surfaces pose a real hazard.**
- **Are there places where fingers, feet or clothes can get caught or pinched? Moving parts should be inaccessible; narrow angles that could trap clothes and protruding screws and nails are other hazards. All surfaces should be smoothly finished.**
- **The arrangement of equipment is also important. Swings, for example, need a large surrounding area so children approaching other equipment are not at risk of being hit.**
- **Playgrounds should be checked regularly for animal excrement, broken glass, and other hazards. Open sand-pits, such as are found in playgrounds and school yards, are often used by cats as giant litterboxes. You may prefer to restrict younger children to your own sandbox, and keep it covered when not in use.**
- **Even with the best design, safe usage is up to you. Dress your child appropriately: shoes with treads that grip well, and no dangling strings, necklaces or scarves that could catch on equipment.** *Preschoolers need adult guidance and supervision to use playground equipment safely.*

Lynn Haines, a professor of early childhood education at Centennial College in Scarborough, Ontario, agrees that kids do better, both physically and mentally, when they're enjoying lots of lively play. "Children need the opportunity to experience things—check them out through all

When Child's Play Is Adult Business: A Consumer Guide to Safer Playspaces **is available from the Canadian Institute of Child Health, 885 Meadowlands Dr. E., Suite 512, Ottawa, Ont. K2C 3N2.The complete guidelines:** *CSA Guidelines on Playground Construction, Design and Manufacture,* **are available from CSA Standard Sales, 178 Rexdale Blvd., Rexdale, Ont. M9W 1R3. If your local park needs improvements, you might want to send a copy to your municipal Parks and Recreation department, and urge them to make the necessary changes.**

the senses. If a child is learning to climb, he has to put a lot of pieces together to accomplish this. A lot of thought goes into the attempt toward physical action."

According to Haines, active play also helps kids become more sure of themselves. "Some children, at three, are timid in the playground, but if you see children who are confident in their bodies, those are the ones who have been allowed to challenge themselves physically."

Obviously, the best place for physical play is outside. "Children get cabin fever," says Haines, "and they need natural light and outdoor air. Their cognitive and mental alertness decreases and their eating, sleeping and coping skills are all affected if they don't get out."

Just ask Nathalie Depippo, mother of five-year-old Kurtis, three-year-old Monique and baby Kendra. She says that, although it's hard getting three little children dressed and out of the house, especially in the winter, "if we don't go outside to play, the day is hell. Inside, by noon they'll be at each other's throats, but outside they're totally different people. I don't know what it is, maybe the space, but they relate to each other differently when they're outside playing."

If active play is so important for kids, what about organized sports? While some kids this age might enjoy a low-key team sport, Orlick points out that this kind of play, with its fixed rules and set structure, doesn't invite creativity the way that free play does. Each time Kurtis Depippo plays "hockey" on his blocked-off driveway, for example, he's reinventing the game. Sometimes there's a basketball involved, sometimes there's someone playing in a ride-on toy near the sidelines. Often, a crew of neighbourhood kids draw with chalk not far from centre ice. But no matter what goes on, Kurtis and his friends can't break the rules—because there are none.

On a frigid November Saturday, a round of Nerfball soccer in the hallway or a wiggle through a family-room obstacle course might be all a parent can manage. And that's just fine. You can find opportunities for spontaneous active play all over the place, if you remember to look. "Parents can tie play to small chunks of time," suggests Orlick. He recalls a busy day when he had lots of chores to do. His then five-year-old daughter and her friend really wanted him to play with them. As he swept the kitchen floor, he grabbed the broom, hopped on and invited the girls to join him. They whirled around the house on the broomstick for a few minutes. Says Orlick, "It took maybe thirty-five seconds, but they were thrilled. It was the highlight of their day." He pauses and adds, "It was the highlight of my day too."

This section is by Cathie Kryczka,
guest contributor to "Steps & Stages."

"CAN I PLAY WITH SADIE?":
MAKING FRIENDS

S ETH AND KATIE WERE NEIGHBOURS. The summer they were three, they both longed for a playmate. Seth trailed hopefully after his big brother's friends. Katie begged daily to visit her cousins, across town. Their mothers put two and two together and started arranging play dates.

But friendship, they discovered, doesn't always happen instantly. Seth and Katie wanted to play together—but they had some things to work out. Seth didn't want to play house; Katie found his dress-up masks too scary. Neither liked letting the other be in charge of their pretend-play plots. Tears and stormy scenes were distressingly frequent.

"Playing co-operatively is a very complex skill," explains Katrina Hughes, co-ordinator of Ryerson Polytechnic University's Early Learning Centre, in Toronto. "There is so much to learn: the social niceties of sharing, taking turns, figuring our who takes the lead—the whole system of rules that have to do with relating to others."

Yet friendship becomes so important in this age-group that children will often endure quite a lot of conflict in order to experience the rewards of togetherness. What do children get from their friends that they don't get from their family or caregivers?

"What do *you* get from friendships with other adults?" asks Linda Squires, who has taught in elementary schools for fifteen years and is currently teaching junior and senior kindergarten. "You get validation of your own life experience, a relationship with an equal, the pleasure of shared interests."

"Developmentally," adds Hughes, "this is part of a child's readiness to move beyond himself and his family (which he sees largely as an extension of himself) into the larger world. The child is becoming more aware of others and their potential."

BOSSYBOOTS

Jessica, age five, has invited another five-year-old girl over to play. "I'm going to be the mom," she announces, "and you're the baby." Her playmate resists: "I always have to be the baby." "Well," counters Jessica, "if you won't be the baby then you can go home because I don't want to play with you."

"I call her a little bossyboots," admits Jessica's mother. "She always has to be in charge."

The key to helping your bossy child is in respecting her strengths—her assertiveness and leadership—while modelling the kind of consideration and understanding for others that you want her to learn. Some suggestions:

- Praise co-operative behaviour. Try to overlook verbal bossiness and watch for times when your child is sharing control. Then, let him know how pleased you are: "I really liked that you let Connor choose his own truck to play with—see how happy he is!" When your child sees how positively you and other children react to his more consider- ate behaviour, he will be encouraged to keep it up.
- Don't confuse assertiveness with aggressiveness. The child who tries to physically force other children to do the things he wants has stepped over the line and adults need to quickly intervene and help with problem-solving.the
- Teach empathy. Pat Tretjak, supervisor, says that at the Sheridan College childcare centre the staff try to help the children understand others' feelings ("Brittany is sad because she wants to play with you but she doesn't want to be the baby") and to find solutions that allow everyone to win ("Could one of you be the mommy and one of you be the daddy, and you could use a doll for the baby?").

Some children, it seems, are "born to socialize" and enter the social whirl of the preschool years effortlessly. Others may be less comfortable in their relationships with other children. Can parents help their preschoolers make friends?

"Parents and teachers can help," says Hughes. "But they don't always have to. If a child doesn't have many friends, but is content, that's okay. Some children, like some adults, enjoy spending time on their own, and it's important to respect that. But if a child is lonely or unhappy about not having playmates, that's different."

First, parents can make sure the opportunity is there. "I usually suggest activities that are fairly unstructured," says Hughes. "Swimming lessons, for example, don't really give the children much opportunity to interact. Try something like a playgroup or a trip to the park with another family, instead. The child may need to just watch at first, until she feels ready. You can't push it."

Squires describes how she helps a "shy" child link up with other children in her classroom. "I'll invite the child to play with me," she says. "We'll set up an activity on the carpet and eventually another child will wander over and join in. Once they're both involved in the play, I 'sneak out the back door.'"

Parents at home can follow a similar strategy to help new friends enjoy each other. At first, they will probably need your help in structuring the situation. Hughes and Squires both observe that children tend to connect around concrete activities: they do something together, rather than sitting around making small talk. A craft activity, a special outing, or making and eating a snack together will help take the awkwardness out of the first couple of get-togethers.

When conflicts do arise, your services as a mediator will help them learn negotiating skills. "I try to help the kids solve their own problems," says Squires. "I'll ask, 'What can we do so that you'll both be happy? How can we share fairly?' They will often come up with good solutions if I intervene early, before they're too angry." The lesson—that friends can disagree, get mad at each other, and still be friends—may need to be reinforced many times in the coming years.

Like adults, children have their own personalities, and compatibility plays a definite role in the course of their friendships. "Some kids are

MAKING FRIENDS WITH THE NEW BABY

Preschoolers are often fascinated with a new baby in the family. They're eager to make friends, but not really sure how to play with someone so little. Parents can help babies and "big kids" make friends by teaching their preschoolers simple, safe games that both can enjoy:

- In the early days, teach your preschooler that babies like to look at faces and clear patterns, but that they can only see things well about a foot or so away. Lying face to face on a blanket, smiling, singing and showing the baby interesting toys are good newborn "games."
- Preschoolers *always* want to hold the baby, yet it's hard for them to do so comfortably and safely. A favourite method is to sit them on a couch or big chair with a pillow on their lap, then lay the baby on the pillow.
- Separate out the toys that are safe for the baby, so your preschooler knows what's okay to give the baby once she can grasp and mouth things.
- Teach your child a gentle action song that she can do with the baby, moving the baby's hands or feet as she recites. (Supervise carefully at first to make sure she knows the difference between gently moving the baby's arms and wrenching them!) The baby will soon come to recognize and respond to "their" song.
- Help your child learn how the baby shows what she likes, and point out the signs that she especially likes *him*: "Do you see how her eyes go all round and she stares at you when you sing that? She really likes that!" or "Listen to that gurgle! She thinks you're wonderful!" It's hard not to like someone who's crazy about *you*!
- If the baby becomes upset, gently rescue your child. Try not to make him feel that he did something wrong or the baby doesn't like him. A more neutral explanation, like "Uh-oh, he's probably tired" or "Maybe he's hungry now" is less discouraging.

like magnets—they instantly attract," observes Squires. "Others seem to be like oil and water." If your child's new playmate is a "kindred spirit," you probably won't have to hover over their play for long—they'll be off in their own world.

Seth and Katie, on the other hand, never really did "click." Once the fall came, and they were both off to school, they rarely asked to play together. But that experience of getting to know a new person and finding common ground may have been better preparation for entering a classroom full of new children, than playing exclusively with their "best friends."

"The process of learning how to make friends and get along with other people is so crucial," reflects Hughes. "It's a skill we need throughout our lives." And really, it all starts with working out who gets to be the princess first, and who will wear the black cape.

ALONE BUT NOT LONELY: SOLITARY PLAY

Y OU WERE PROBABLY RAISED to believe that eavesdropping was a bad thing, but try hiding around a corner and listening to your preschooler next time he or she is playing alone. You'll hear intimate conversations with inanimate objects, amazing flights of imagination and sometimes embarrassingly accurate imitations of parents—and you'll learn a great deal about your child.

Developing social skills that help us get along with others is certainly an important part of the preschooler's development. But solitary play teaches other, equally important skills. Author Teresa Amabile writes in her book, *Growing Up Creative*, about the importance of solitary play in developing creativity: "It is through this kind of play that children learn, challenge themselves, and discover their strongest interests... Even if your son is having some trouble figuring out how to do something, give him a little time and space to figure it out himself. Even if your daughter is using a toy in the 'wrong' way, leave her alone. Maybe she's just discovered a new 'right' way to do it!"

Amabile bases her comments on a long-term study of homes and families of creative children, compared to families where the children were considered less creative. One of the important attitudes of parents of creative children included the belief that "a child should have time to think, daydream, and goof off." In "less creative" families, the emphasis tended to be on scheduled, structured, and group activities.

"But my child doesn't like to play alone!" parents will sometimes say. Every child has his or her own level of sociability, but parents of preschoolers can take steps to help their children develop the skills of playing and entertaining themselves.

Jan Jacklin, the mother of Charlie (seven), Adam (five) and Jessica (two), finds that having appropriate toys available is important.

FUN FOR ONE: TOYS FOR SOLITARY PLAY
Toys that invite a child to enjoy his own creativity and imagination help make "playing by yourself" a pleasure:

- Dolls, big and small: baby dolls, puppets, "playsets" with figures (like Playmobil), little plastic animals and stuffed big ones
- Construction toys: like Duplo, wooden blocks, and (for older preschoolers) Lego
- Craft supplies: Put together a box of things she can manage without (much) help: white, coloured and cardboard paper; washable markers; a glue stick; and cool stuff to glue (feathers, leaves, confetti, sequins); stickers, stamps and washable ink pads
- Play-Doh and gadgets to go with it
- A children's tape recorder, with story and music tapes and a blank tape for recording herself
- Books: Keep the picture books on a low shelf where he can browse easily, and you may be surprised how much time he spends "reading" to himself.
- A private space: Many preschoolers don't like to get too far away from Mom or Dad (like in a separate bedroom), but she might love it if you pulled out the armchair to make a little cave behind it, or threw a tablecloth over the coffee table to make a tent. Perfect for daydreaming or quiet make-believe.

"So many toys can't be played with alone," she points out. "All the board games and many of the toys need others to play with. So we make sure we have Play-Doh, puzzles, dolls, blocks or building sets—things that work with one. I even taught them to play solitaire at an early age!"

Another requirement, she feels, is the right space. "Adam, for example, has his own room, and that's his space where he can play alone and set up things the way he wants it. Even if the boys shared a room, I would give them each a corner that would be their private spot," she says.

But a private playspace doesn't have to be in a bedroom. Jan often brings out Play-Doh or building blocks and clears a "workspace" on the kitchen table for Adam to enjoy. Bathtime is another opportunity for solitary play.

"With children Adam's age, you don't have to stay with them all the time—although I do stay close by—and they can have a great time playing in the water if you provide some toys. I don't call it bathtime, I call it waterplay time!"

Finally, Jan stresses the importance of helping a young child develop the skills he or she needs to play alone. "I'm a firm believer that children need to learn to make their own amusements. So I would help by setting the scene for them, and then just 'butting out.'"

For example, Jan would take Adam along to the park and say, "I'm going to sit here with Jessica, and you can play on the climber. Is it going to be a boat today? Or a fort?" That little nudge was usually enough to get Adam's imagination going. Indoors, Jan might bring out the Lego blocks and ask Adam what he wanted to build—and ask him to show it to her once he finished. That let him know that she wasn't going to be helping him with the construction, but that she was interested in and ready to admire his accomplishments.

While it is relatively easy to provide a private space and appropriate toys for a child's solitary play at home, young children who spend most of their days in a group care situation also need private playtime.

Pat Tretjak, supervisor of the Sheridan College childcare centre, says, "We allow the child to make the choice to play alone, and we help them to tell the other children that's what they want to do." The staff doesn't insist that children share the toys but instead encourages them to say something like "I'm playing with this by myself now, you can play with it when I'm finished."

Tretjak adds that daycare staff must be aware of the need for solitary play. "I call it 'downtime.' It requires a lot of energy to be with a group all day, and they need that opportunity to play alone as well. There should be an area set up where they can go, a cosy book corner or a rocking chair or a table where one child can play with a puzzle."

It can be a challenge to create the right atmosphere for your child's solitary play, but it will continue to be an important part of his or her development for many years to come.

MISS POLLY HAD A DOLLY: THE VALUE OF DOLLS

HE DOLLS IN NURSERY TWO preschool are in bad shape. Since the new hospital corner was set up, they have been sick or injured most of the time. They lie in a row on the mattress, covered with dozens of Band-Aids.

"What's wrong with this one?" I ask the three little girls who cluster around the patients.

"She had a fluoride test," one says ominously. "She had to have it in her ear, because she wouldn't open her mouth."

The dolls are rearranged, given numerous needles, and dosed with medicine. Then a tiny doll is brought to me.

"Put this under your shirt," commands Sara. "You're going to have a baby."

I oblige, and when the baby's birthday is announced, I bring her out.

"Not that way!" The girls giggle in unison. "You have to lie down! Now the doctor pulls it out."

I'm ceremoniously offered my new baby girl, completely hidden in a blanket. But new perils arise. She's sick, too. The doctors huddle around, consulting. Finally, the diagnosis: "She has a cavity."

Dolls have a special place in the world of toys, because they so clearly represent people. Through dolls, a child can explore human relationships and roles. Often, the doll stands for the child, who can then try out the adult's role (parent, doctor, teacher). Kids can work through past experiences and try to understand unfamiliar aspects of their world by re-creating these events for their dolls. (It was easy to guess that one of the girls at nursery school had just been to the dentist, and another had a new baby sister.)

"Dolls encourage an elaborate kind of play," says Margaret De Corte, a developmental psychologist at the University of Ottawa who

---

BUT IS AN ACTION FIGURE A DOLL?

If, by age four, little boys are often reluctant to play with dolls, they have no such qualms about the ubiquitous "action figure"—the uglier and more grotesquely muscled, it seems, the better. These "dolls" seem to inspire, mainly, various kinds of crashing and blowing up—but they *can* also provide some of the imaginative and social benefits of more traditional dolls. Some suggestions for encouraging a more varied, creative kind of action-figure play:

- Buy a "nice" figure. Make sure your son has at least one or two figures that are relatively young, friendly, and human-looking: maybe Luke Skywalker, Wesley from *Star Trek*, or Enzo from *Reboot*...They more easily double as a confidant, bedtime companion or dental patient.
- Add props that suggest imaginative play: a field hospital, a campfire and frying pan (even superheroes, presumably, have to eat), a spaceship, a treasure map. Better still, make them together.
- Recast them. See if this will fly: "I've got a funny idea. Let's make a family of figures!" He may start off casting the mother, father and children as a joke—but odds are, he'll go on to actually play "house" with them. (My own three boys once cast the main characters from the novel *Lord of the Rings* entirely out of action figures, based primarily on relative height. They apparently had no trouble at all seeing Spiderman as an elvish prince and Penguin as a dwarf.)

---

also gives parenting courses and workshops. "They stimulate a lot of discussion, social interaction and fantasy."

De Corte notes that while two-year-olds may put a doll in a carriage, or wash its hair in the bath, what we think of as "true pretend play" doesn't usually emerge until closer to age three, when "children develop a wonderful ability to start sequencing events." Now the child is able to re-create a routine such as bedtime with his doll, or invent and sustain a rudimentary "plot."

Sometimes a favourite doll becomes a special friend. In *Your Child at*

Play: Three to Five Years, Marilyn Segal and Don Adcock write: "As the doll babies mirror the wishes and fears of the children, they become companions, for it is easy to make friends with someone who is just like you...these companions are always ready to play the role of 'extra.' A child who plays doctor can count on them to be patients. A child who wants to be a teacher has a ready-made classroom of pupils."

What makes a good doll for a preschooler?

For the youngest children, the best dolls are probably soft and cuddly, simple and easy to carry. Segal and Adcock note that dolls most likely to be adopted as special friends tend to be soft and floppy, with "big eyes and a sad expression." But children soon develop their own taste. As long as a doll matches your child's ability (is she dextrous enough to work the mechanism to make the hair grow?) and your budget, her own preference is your best guide.

Experts encourage us to give our boys access to dolls as well. After all, we want them to develop social skills and nurturing abilities, too. "Boy" dolls like the Cabbage Patch Kids, introduced in the mid-1980s, have strong appeal for many little guys. But other boys either never show much interest, or learn quickly enough from television and peers to avoid dolls as "girls' stuff." Should we be concerned?

"Children are telling us what they are preoccupied with, what their current interests are, by how they choose to play," says De Corte. "So I think it's important to leave the choice to them. Given a broad choice of different toys and playmates, children will experiment—but they'll favour the type of play that is important to them. If we try to force a certain kind of play, then we're not accepting what the child is communicating, and we're ultimately sending 'You're not okay' messages to our children."

Some boys may reject dolls, but choose other toys to fill the same role. There's many a favourite bear who's been tenderly tucked into bed and fed breakfast in the morning. In my family, a tiny Lego man named Merdley was a favourite for several months. He was always getting into trouble, using Lego machinery he wasn't supposed to touch. (Doesn't that sound like a little boy I know!) And puppets appeal to both sexes.

Back at the nursery school, a quiet little boy has had a monkey puppet on his hand all morning. He wore it while linking together a circus train, and then gave it a ride in the caboose. He wore it while building with blocks, cumbersome though it was. Now it's clean-up time, and the monkey is picking up blocks in its mouth and carrying them to the shelves.

"My animal's helping," he announces to the teacher.

"Isn't your monkey clever, to carry blocks in his mouth like that!" she enthuses. And together the three of them head over for circle, where the monkey will no doubt sing along—just in case his friend is feeling a bit shy.

PORTRAIT OF AN ARTIST: EXPLORING
PENCIL, BRUSH AND PAPER

OUR-YEAR-OLD NOAH IS ENGROSSED in a complex drawing project. He works intently, with purpose. He makes a number of forms, most of them circles. He makes a cross inside one. He fills two others with dots and connects them with a jaggedy lightning-line. Lines radiate out from one form like hair; and a loopy line like a strung-out spiral circles around the page. Although some might call this "scribbling," it's a long way from the random, uncontrolled scribbling Noah did at two.

Wendy Spengler, a family service social worker with the Halton Children's Aid, often uses children's artwork in assessment and therapy programs, because it reveals so much about their development and emotions. She notes that children's so-called scribbling follows a definite developmental progression: "They will usually start with lines, then add curves and spirals. Somewhere around age three, most children start to make enclosed figures: simple forms like circles or squares, crosses, etc. Later still they combine these shapes and scribbles to make designs, for example, intersecting lines placed inside a circle. But it's not until age four or five that most children will deliberately try to make a picture of something recognizable."

Melba Rabinowitz, an early childhood specialist in St. John's, Newfoundland, who has a special interest in the emergence of children's writing and drawing, adds, "This is a universal developmental process. Around the world, children emerge with these same shapes on their own, whether they're using fancy markers or a stick in the mud."

Rabinowitz urges parents and teachers to respect these early efforts: "If adults correct children, ask them to draw it 'right,' erase it and do it again, they may undermine the child's development." As artist Sally Warner, author of *Encouraging the Artist in Your Child*, writes, scrib-

---

BEYOND "WHAT IS IT?"

"Asking 'What is it?' is discouraging to a child because it suggests that he's done it wrong," Wendy Spengler explains. She adds that, in any case, many four-year-olds are not yet creating "pictorial" drawings: *"Young children are into the pleasure of scribbling, rather than the final product."*

If "What is it?" is an artistic faux-pas, what are more supportive responses to a child's artwork?

- **Try to find something specific you genuinely like.** Perhaps that bright yellow is one of your favourite colours. Perhaps you can admire the intricacy of those spiral loops. You can also simply describe, enthusiastically, what you see: "So many beautiful, bright colours!"
- **Appreciate the effort or the enjoyment rather than the content.** "You worked for a really long time on this picture!" tells the child you respect his efforts.
- **Ask open-ended questions.** If you'd like to learn more about your *child's* view of her picture try questions like, "Can you tell me about your drawing?" or "You've used lots of red. What kind of feeling does red have for you?" Some children will like to have you write down what they say about their picture, either on the back or on a separate title card.

---

bling "is not practising for 'real' drawing... It's already real." She feels strongly that, when adults try to hurry (or "help") a child's drawing development, "we are sacrificing something precious and unique in each child to our own vanity." So while we may want to show a child how to use a new medium (potato printing), and we'll certainly want to teach appropriate limits (scribble on paper, not on the tabletop), we should resist that urge to add in some eyes or "improve" an arrangement.

In her own time, then, your child will progress to figurative drawing. Usually she will attempt familiar objects from her everyday world, with the most popular being representations of people or animals (they'll look very similar at this stage). Spengler describes the classic early drawing, known as the "tadpole drawing" (usually a person), which starts with a

HEADS, BODIES AND LEGS

Once your child can draw a basic person, he might enjoy this game:

- The first person draws a head, then folds back the paper so only enough of the drawing shows to guide the placement of the body.
- The next person draws the body, and again folds the paper.
- A third person (or the first again, if there's just the two of you) draws the feet.

Open up the paper, and *voila!*: a very funny-looking creature. This is a game kids of all ages like, and because the goal is to be funny rather than "accurate," beginning and advanced drawers can mix and match happily.

circle with a few features (often just eyes and a mouth), and then sprouts arms and one or two legs right out of the head. It's really fun to watch a child expand this basic drawing by adding on more complex features and a body: if you save a series of examples over the next couple of years you'll see a marked artistic evolution that reflects both your child's growing control over her drawing tools and her cognitive development.

Sally Warner notes that children develop their own repertory of "symbols," which mature over time much as the tadpole-man does. Your child will develop her own way of representing images which are important to her: pets, houses, trucks or trees. Melba Rabinowitz has observed the same use of personal symbols in children's "prewriting": a child will make distinctive letter-like marks over and over.

Around senior kindergarten age, children's drawing often becomes more conventional. Suddenly, there's a proliferation of houses with rainbows over them, or page after page of

FURTHER READING
Encouraging the Artist in Your Child (Even If You Can't Draw), by Sally Warner, St. Martin's Press (Canadian distributor McClelland & Stewart), 1989. Lots of tips for helping kids follow their own artistic star. Part One is geared to children ages two to five; Part Two is for six- to ten-year-olds.

Spiderman. While these drawings may seem to lack originality, Warner observes that children at this stage get a lot of satisfaction out of being able to replicate their drawings.

"I remember in senior kindergarten my son and his friends went through a Batman phase," says Marie Woods. "One of them was quite advanced in drawing, and for a couple of weeks Ben came home every day with one (or more!) bats that Miles had drawn for him. Then one afternoon he decided he had to learn to do it for himself. He went through an entire pad of paper, drawing bat after bat, and bursting into tears more than once. I could hardly stand it. But he finally was able to draw a bat to his own satisfaction, and he was really, really pleased with himself." As long as the impetus to copy comes from the child rather than an adult, says Warner, it's probably serving a purpose in that child's development.

Whether your child is fascinated, like Noah, with lines and patterns, or more interested in exploring colour; whether she makes pictures of flowers or Sailor Moon or secret treasure maps or who-knows-whats, her art is uniquely her own. "If they are not criticized, children are very expressive with their art," notes Spengler. "The themes and colours they choose have meaning for them. Their pictures give a sense of how they're seeing their world."

TV: THE NEVER-ENDING STORY:
HOW TO TAME THE TUBE

ORGAN IS A BUSY FOUR-YEAR-OLD who can barely sit still long enough to eat dinner. But look at her now. Eyes unblinking, body motionless, she seems oblivious to the world around her. A coma? No. Television.

It's spooky, the hypnotic power television has over many kids. No wonder we worry about how much they watch and whether it's good for them.

Yet few of us are willing to pull the plug altogether. Cookie Monster is too loveable. Nature shows give kids glimpses of animal life that no zoo could replicate. And, admit it, that half-hour of peace while you're trying to prepare dinner is too tempting. For most parents, then, the issue is taming, not banishing, the tube. Can television be a positive influence on our kids?

The Children's Broadcast Institute has been working since 1974 to encourage high-quality children's programming in Canada, and to help us understand how television influences children. Executive director David Schatzky has lots of good suggestions to help us use television wisely. "The dangers of too much TV are like the dangers of too much anything," he says. "Your life is out of balance. A child who watches a great deal of television is not getting enough exercise, creative activity, social interaction.

"The key thing is to establish your role as limiter," Schatzky suggests. "The actual limit is up to you. But by setting it, you're establishing the comparative value of other activities, like playing together."

Some families have found a few ground rules that help. "We never have the TV on as background," says Alan West. "If we're not actually watching it, it's off." Protests at turn-off time are often avoided with "a quick trigger-finger. You have to hit the button right at the end of the

VIOLENT TV, VIOLENT TOYS

It doesn't take parents long to figure out that TV programming and toy marketing are inextricably connected. And while there are numerous issues to grapple with here—like sexual stereotyping and the ethics of marketing to children—it's probably the promotion of violent entertainment that worries everyone the most. Numerous studies have found that children who watch a lot of violent programming behave more aggressively and see the world as more dangerous. After all, they are bombarded with images of "bad guys," routine violence and glamorized armed conflict.

Dr. Joanna Santa Barbara is a child psychiatrist and vice-chair of Canadian Physicians for the Prevention of Nuclear War. While she champions children's need to choose their play themes freely, she also stresses, "'Scripting' by the media is very strong, and has a great influence on play apart from children's inner needs. Children watch violent cartoons, and then they re-create these violent scenes with the corresponding toys."

What to do? Some parents place an out-and-out ban on anything violent. Some don't worry about it. Most of us make a brave attempt to find sensible limits, drawing lines that may seem more arbitrary than logical: no toy guns, but a knight's sword is okay. No live action violence, but cartoons are okay. Well, maybe just *Star Wars* because I loved that as a kid. It seems, sometimes, like ineffective waffling, but it *is* still worthwhile. It's not so much *which* shows and toys you allow, but that you don't allow violent themes to take over either the toy box or the airwaves. By limiting and delaying exposure to violent material, and providing appealing alternatives, you can foster a richer variety of imaginative play.

show. If the kids get a glimpse of the next cartoon they're desperate to watch it, too."

Parents also need to consider the appropriateness and quality of programs. Says Schatzky, "Some content is confusing, overstimulating, or scary for young children."

Violence is a particular issue for many parents (see box, above). It certainly gets harder to veto shows as our kids grow, but in the early

RESOURCES
Your Child and TV. A booklet available free from the Children's Broadcast Institute. Membership in the Institute costs $20 a year. Write to: The Children's Broadcast Institute, 234 Eglinton Avenue East, Suite 405, Toronto, Ontario M4P 1K5.

Television and Your Children. An excellent booklet from TV Ontario. To order send $5 plus $1 for shipping to: TV Ontario Marketing, Box 200, Station Q, Toronto, Ontario M4T 2T1.

Who's Calling the Shots? How to Respond Effectively to Children's Fascination with War Play and War Toys, by Nancy Carlsson-Paige and Diane E. Levin, New Society Publishers, 1990.

preschool years parents hold the cards. "We don't let Sandy turn on the set and randomly flip channels," says one mom. "We tune in to a particular show. This also allows us to keep her in blissful ignorance of what she's missing. I have no qualms about editing the *TV Guide* until she can read it herself." Some families restrict their children's early TV exposure to public television channels (blessedly ad-free). Even so, moderation is the key word. "Because the shows are so good, you let your child watch at an earlier age," says Susan Newman, mother of two. "You think, "It's Polkaroo, it's Fred [Penner]—what can be the harm? But by three, those shows are old hat and he wants cartoons—and you've already established the habit of two hours a day. Now what?"

Things get even more complicated when there's an older sibling at home. "Joe (my youngest) at two is watching things that Dan (now five) hadn't even heard of at that age," laments Susan. "It worries me, but I'm not sure what to do about it."

Schatzky has some reassurance for her: "When kids have a parent—or an older sibling—to mediate a show, then the scary or overwhelming parts are easier for them to handle." If Joe sees Dan laughing at a cartoon monster, then he's not likely to find it so frightening. A parent, of course, can interpret and reassure more directly: "That's just pretend. It's a story, like in your books."

Indeed, watching with our children is strongly advised by everyone who studies kids and television. Convenient as it may be to use TV time to accomplish our own tasks, our participation is extremely valuable. We can extend the benefit of shows we enjoy: make Mr. Dressup's craft together or listen to a Sharon, Lois and Bram album. We can help unravel a complicated story-line. And we can start to teach kids to think critically about what they see: "I notice the bad guys were all really ugly. Do you think that's true in real life?" or "I wonder if elves would really appear in our kitchen if you ate that cereal?"

A timely question can lead you interesting places: my five-year-old and I have been talking a lot about the possibility of life after death and the nature of the human spirit. And to think, it all started with *Ghostbusters*!

STORIES, STOP SIGNS AND LOVE LETTERS: SETTING THE STAGE FOR A LOVE OF READING

WHEN MY THREE SISTERS and I were children, one of our family's Saturday rituals was the drive into town to visit the library. We piled into our station wagon, loaded up the back with dozens of books, and once we were home again, usually spent most of the afternoon lounging around, reading the books we'd checked out—children and adults alike.

The legacy of those lazy Saturday afternoons: a family of readers.

In some ways, of course, my parents had it easier—we lived on a farm (no malls within walking distance), we only got a couple of TV stations, and Nintendo hadn't yet been invented. Parents today who want to help their children become good and enthusiastic readers face tougher challenges. But it's still possible to create a "literate environment" for your preschooler that will set the stage for a lifelong enjoyment of reading.

Brenda Mayes, mother of two and a primary teacher since 1980, suggests that children become ready to read only after they have "developed a love of books and an understanding of the concept of reading."

"Reading to young children is the biggie," Mayes explains. "It's important because they are with you; it's a nice, cosy, happy time; and they're making positive associations with reading. At the same time, they're hearing the language, and developing a more sophisticated vocabulary. And the repetition is important. Parents get tired of reading the same book over and over, but children need that—that's how they come to recognize the words."

Elaine Lum's son, Lucas, has been read to since before his first birthday. "Not just at bedtime, but anytime," she says. At four, Lucas would often ask for the same picture book every night. "We'd read it until he

THE EARLY READER

If early exposure to books is good, isn't early reading even better? Not necessarily. While being read *to* is wonderful for preschoolers, trying to teach them reading skills may backfire.

Claire Zeller, co-ordinator of gifted programs with the Peel Board of Education, cautions parents against what he calls "hot-housing" their preschoolers by trying to push them into reading. If the child is not ready and not interested, the most likely outcome is negative feelings about reading, he points out. And who is likely to get more out of reading in the long term—the six-year-old who already has a library of favourite books and can't wait to learn to read, or the six-year-old who *can* read, but avoids it like the plague?

But some preschoolers actually teach themselves to read, or demand that you help them ("What's this word? What do 'T' and 'H' together say?"). You couldn't hold them back if you tried! This is a very different scenario from a child who is pushed prematurely into reading. As long as the child is leading the process, says Zeller, go ahead and support his efforts. But keep on reading aloud, as well: he needs the complexity and richness of the stories you read to him, as well as simple stories he can manage on his own.

had it almost memorized," Elaine recalls. "I would hear him saying it under his breath along with me, and eventually I would leave blanks, and he'd finish the line. When he had 'mastered' the story, he'd turn to something new." Then, when he was nearly five, Lucas saw a video of the classic children's novel *The Lion, the Witch, and the Wardrobe*. "When I told him that the movie was from a book, he immediately wanted to read it. I was afraid it would be too difficult for him, but he loved it. We've read practically the whole series now." Lucas can't actually read anything but his own name yet, but he is already passionate about books.

Elizabeth Hudson, another primary teacher with ten years of experience and three young children of her own, suggests ways to enhance the "read-to-me" experience.

"Have them sit with you so they can see the pages as you read," she says, "and talk about what you see in the pictures as well as reading the text on the page. Of course, they do go through stages when all they want is the text—and it better be word-for-word or they'll get upset. Sometimes if you follow along with your finger as you read, it helps them make the connection between the written and spoken word. But the emphasis should be on making storytime an enjoyable, pleasurable experience."

Some preschoolers, in Hudson's experience, prefer to approach reading through writing. They may begin with scribbles or random letters, but they can tell you quite clearly what the scribbles mean. Then they may add initial letters, or break the scribbles up into words. Others will ask you to write for them—perhaps adding captions to pictures they have done—and will be able to "read" those words back to you.

Other activities Mayes recommends: pointing out road and store signs during family drives, taking old labels (from, for example, soup cans) with you to the grocery store and asking the children to find the matching item, going for a walk and collecting items to be labelled at home, playing "I Spy" using initial sounds, singing songs and reciting nursery rhymes.

Hudson stresses: "They've got to see *you* reading, even if it's just a letter from a relative." Better still, show them from your example that reading is enjoyable as well as useful. When they see you buried in a novel or magazine, they learn that reading can be a lifelong pleasure.

She suggests encouraging the children to participate in your own writing activities, as well. They can, for example, suggest items to be

READING RESOURCES

The Reading Solution: Making Your Child a Reader for Life, by Paul Kropp, Random House, 1993

Literacy Begins at Birth, by Marjorie V. Fields, Fisher Books, 1989.

Michele Landsberg's Guide to Children's Books, by Michele Landsberg, Penguin, 1986

The New Read-Aloud Handbook, by Jim Trelease, Penguin, 1989

added to the shopping list or dictate a letter to Grandma or Santa. Children also love to get notes—leave them on the pillow at bedtime, or tucked into the snack they take to nursery school—even if they have to ask someone else to read them.

Another project, suggested by Mayes, is to create books with your child. "A Day in the Life of Laura," for example, could include photos (or drawings) with captions dictated by Laura. Other books could be on specific themes: animals, things I like, colours, a vacation, etc. A "multi-sensory" book could include different scents (dab the page with vanilla or perfume) or fabrics with different textures (fake fur, corduroy, etc.).

Mayes emphasizes that all these activities should be fun for both child and parent. "One of the axioms of learning is that it's easier to learn in a relaxed, accepting atmosphere than in a tense, 'expecting' environment," she explains. "It's also easier to learn new skills when they are related to real-life experiences than when they are taught in isolation."

Children become interested in learning to read at different ages. But creating an atmosphere at home where books and the stories within them are always available and fun to read will give any child a head start into the world of literacy.

Recommended Reading

IN ADDITION TO THE BOOKS on specific topics listed in the text, we've found the following volumes especially helpful in understanding, guiding and just plain living with preschoolers:

Becoming the Parent You Want to Be: A Sourcebook of Strategies for the First Five Years, by Laura Davis and Janis Keyser, Broadway Books, 1997.

How to Read Your Child Like a Book: Learn to Interpret Your Child's Behavior during the First Six Years, So You Can Be a More Effective Parent, by Lynn Weiss, Simon & Schuster, 1997.

Parenting by Heart: How to Connect with Your Kids in the Face of Too Much Advice, Too Many Pressures, and Never Enough Time, by Dr. Ron Taffel, Addison-Wesley, 1991.

Raising Your Spirited Child: A Guide for Parents Whose Child Is More Intense • Sensitive • Perceptive • Persistent • Energetic, by Mary Sheedy Kurcinka, HarperCollins, 1991.

Your Baby and Child: From Birth to Age Five, by Penelope Leach, Alfred A. Knopf, revised 1989.